KRIS,

BEST WISHES FOR AN "ENERGIZED" 2016!

ENJOY

WORKING IN SYNC

How Eleven Dartmouth Athletes Propelled
Their College Sports Experience into
Professional Excellence

WHIT MITCHELL with members of the
CLASS OF '86 DARTMOUTH CREW

Working in Sync: How Eleven Dartmouth Athletes Propelled Their College Sports Experience into Professional Excellence
by Whit Mitchell with members of the class of '86 Dartmouth crew

To purchase copies of *Working in Sync* in large quantities at wholesale prices, please contact Aloha Publishing at alohapublishing@gmail.com or go to WorkinginSyncBook.com.

Cover Design: Cari Campbell, Cari Campbell Design
Interior Design: Nick Zelinger, NZ Graphics
Primary Editor: Stacy Ennis

Print ISBN: 978-1-61206-036-1
eBook ISBN: 978-1-61206-044-6

Library of Congress Control Number: 2013934749

First Printing
Printed in Canada

Published by: AlohaPublishing.com

Working in Sync is dedicated to
my Mum—Shirlee Sanderson Mitchell.

Thanks for persuading me to go out for crew
at South Kent. It was a life changer!

Whitter

Contents

Introduction

When you think back on your life, can you pinpoint what helped shape who you are today? Perhaps it was a person—someone who saw greatness inside of you and helped you discover your worth. Maybe it was a profound experience—something that helped you rediscover the value of life and those around you. For eleven young athletes back in 1982, one of those "life-shaping" times occurred during Dartmouth freshman crew, class of '86. I was their coach, and they were my team.

My experience coaching those freshmen was one of the richest in my entire sports coaching career. So I was thrilled when, nearly thirty years later, the team invited me back to their 25th Dartmouth reunion in Hanover, New Hampshire. As I reconnected with my former athletes, I was amazed at the outstanding success they'd each had, both personally and professionally, and I felt their stories needed to be shared with the world. Months later, *Working in Sync* began as a way to tell the stories of those eleven exceptional Dartmouth crew athletes. But what developed ended up being so much more than simple stories about personal accomplishments; instead, I discovered riveting lessons about success and life.

As I reconnected with each of the athletes and listened to their individual transformative experiences, many of which started in college crew, I began to draw connections between what they learned as college athletes and their successes as professionals. More importantly, as I was deeply engaged in interviewing them for the book, I began to see practical strategies around team dynamics, executive coaching, achieving and living one's values, personal fulfillment, motivation, and, ultimately, personal and professional success. Each of them had a lesson to teach and a story to share that I knew could truly transform anyone looking to make changes in their own lives.

What about you? Have you reached the highest point in your career or do you have goals yet to be accomplished? As a leader, could you better utilize the expertise, knowledge, and engagement of different team members to expand your business? Are there ways you could grow and change that would positively impact those around you? If you could influence others by sharing one aspect of your work life that defines your success, what would it be?

As you read the eleven life stories of these amazing men, you may feel like you're benefiting from your own personal MBA program. But unlike most MBA programs, you'll learn directly from world leaders in business, health care, venture capital, and nonprofit organizations, among other professional insights. From the Forbes Midas List of top tech investors, like Scott Sandell of New Enterprise Associates, to CFO of KickStart International Sam Hartwell, to internationally renowned neurosurgeon Mark Proctor, these stories are not only inspiring and practical but also applicable to nearly any leadership situation. Together, they offer simple tools to create deeper levels of communication and sustained motivation in employees; insights about leadership skills, ideas, and behaviors; and multiple perspectives on what "professional and life success" look like—all of which will have an impact on how you conduct business from this day forward.

Moreover, each story draws connections between what each athlete learned in their college sports experience that they used in their later professional endeavors—and teaches you how to apply the same lessons in your own life, regardless of your industry or location. Each chapter is followed by a set of questions that will empower you to implement transformative life lessons in your day-to-day work and personal experiences, drawn from my thirty years working with world-class business leaders, Fortune 500 companies, and Olympic, professional, and collegiate athletes. In essence, you hold in your hands a powerful multi-lesson business course—a personal MBA—that exceeds status quo professional success. By engaging with the stories and really putting them into practice, you can reach higher levels of success in every aspect of life. If you involve your team in the transformative process by reading the book as a collective group and discussing the learning and insights gained from these real-life success stories, you can also create an opportunity for company-wide success.

Meet the Team

On a warm evening in June of 2011, I was walking down Main Street in Hanover, New Hampshire, on my way to the Canoe Club restaurant where I was to reunite with the eleven Dartmouth freshman athletes of the 1982 rowing team. It'd been twenty-five years since I'd seen these athletes—men, now—and I was anxious and excited to see how they had changed, who they had become in the many years that had passed.

I could see the restaurant in the distance, and as I got closer, I started thinking about the oarsmen, many of whom had never rowed before we first met twenty-eight years ago. During one of our very first team meetings, I remember watching them wander into the old boathouse to marvel at the length and craftsmanship of the sixty-one-foot wooden shells. There was a sense of youthfulness and excitement as they began to introduce themselves to each other, and they could tell that this adventure was going to be something different, something that was more than first imagined, something that would make their Dartmouth College experience memorable.

This group of guys had something different in their approach to this new endeavor than I had seen in my first eight years of coaching. Was it because they were Ivy League? Did I just happen to have one of those groups of athletes that was unique and special? It happens once in a long while as a coach or business leader. You know, that experience in school, camp, a workshop, or in business, where you happen to be part of a really great group of people? You can feel it the very first day you meet and learn about each person. There was something special about this group of guys; I could tell right away.

My mind returning to the present moment, I opened the door to the main entryway and was led to the table I had reserved. I had arrived early so that I would get the chance to greet each of them as they entered the restaurant. As each athlete walked in, I knew I would be able to recognize each of them, even after twenty-five years. It was amazing. They hadn't really changed that much: bellies were a bit bigger and some hair a bit grayer, and their smiles, hugs, and excitement to see each other became more and more infectious. One by one, they came in and sat down for a beer and a story. As I talked to each of them, I learned a bit about what they'd been up to since we were all last together in the spring of 1982:

> **Malcolm McIver,** the coxswain, possessed that drive to compete with an innate ability to push a crew of eight, big, young, and inexperienced oarsmen to get more out of them than they thought they had to give. He is now president and owner of Commerce Properties real-estate investment company in Portland, Oregon.

> **Hans Stander,** the stroke and eight seat, lives in Europe and wasn't able to attend the reunion. I remember him for his

quick wit and determination to be the best at anything he attempted. He's now an infrastructure builder and philanthropic private equity fundraiser, who has created over one million jobs in Russia and five additional countries. His work is known globally.

Garth T. Mark, the seven seat, had warmth for helping others while always being well organized and meticulous for preparation. He lives in New York City and works as the catering and events coordinator for a global, 400-employee ad agency. Before that, he opened a first-of-its-kind boutique espresso bar in New York City.

Scott Sandell, the six seat, had and continues to have a great sense of work ethic, along with a desire to lead with a sense of humor and determination. He is now a general partner at the venture capital firm New Enterprise Associates and is a Forbes Midas List top tech investor.

Wolf-Dietrich Weber, the five seat, didn't realize his own strength and potential until we got to a race in Tennessee in March of 1982. He was strong, powerful, determined, humble, and loved to pull hard. Wolf now works for Google as a principal engineer, innovating new products and processes.

Mike Rich, the four seat, was intrigued by the Far East culture from the day I first met him and was "strong like a bull" on the team. He's now an associate professor of Japanese and Asian Studies and the Japanese program coordinator at Georgetown College in southwest Kentucky. He recently spent a yearlong sabbatical in Japan.

Sam Kinney, the three seat, brought the much-appreciated humor, looseness, and character that helped bring us all together in 1982. He is the cofounder and former executive vice president of FreeMarkets and was able to retire ten years out of the Tuck School of Business.

Charlie Peterson, at six feet six inches, was the number two seat. He was tall, slender, strong, and quietly determined, with a terrific team approach and attitude toward the sport. He now works as an orthopedic surgeon and serves as vice president and board member of the Seattle-based $250-million-a-year company, Proliance Surgeons.

Sam Hartwell, the bowman, was one of two experienced oarsmen coming in from a strong high school crew program. His continued optimistic and fun-loving approach to crew got us all through the tough workouts. He's now the CFO at KickStart International and has helped get three quarters of a million people out of poverty mainly in Kenya, where he lived with his family for three-and-a-half years, just as KickStart was expanding around the globe.

Dan Kollmorgan, alternate, took a risk by switching from football to crew midyear and fought from behind to match the skill of the rest of the team. He was in the freshman four that won a silver medal at the Intercollegiate Rowing Association regatta and was later named captain his senior year. Dan is now a surgical oncologist and lead physician at The Iowa Clinic, a nationally recognized multi-specialty medical group, of which his father is one of the founders.

Mark Proctor, alternate, was the winner of the Marshall Robinson Award for Most Improved Heavyweight Oarsman his junior year at Dartmouth. Mark was not a naturally gifted oarsman but through persistence, determination, and many early morning tank sessions proved his value and strengths on the team. Mark is now an internationally renowned neurosurgeon and head of the Brain Injury Center at Boston Children's Hospital. He believes his role in crew was helpful in getting him into medical school.

* * *

That evening, there was such engagement in the Canoe Club restaurant: connecting, laughing, and smiling. These were grown men hugging and high-fiving, and each time another former athlete walked in, the whole celebration started up again. We'd pull up another chair and another team member and spouse would come in and join the group. And you could tell the spouses were also excited to meet the people they had heard about for years.

The next day, we all met up for a row, but with ten athletes and nine seats, I asked Sam Kinney to row with the lightweight class of '86, also having their class reunion row that weekend. The boat was set, and they quickly challenged their '86 classmates from the lightweight eight to a 1000-meter race. Then began the banter back and forth as the boats left the dock. The families of the oarsmen piled into the launches so they could follow the shells upstream for the race. It was a thrill not only for spouses and kids to see their husband/father do something that he hadn't done for twenty-five years—it brought chills up and down my spine to be back out on the water again with this fine group of very accomplished men. And guess what? They rowed pretty well as they left the dock. Malcolm took them through their paces and a couple of drills to get them working in sync.

Days later, I realized that this reunion had impacted me viscerally, in a way that touched me deeply. They had shared stories of the impact that year of crew had made on them professionally and personally, and I realized I was fortunate to have had such a profound influence on them. On one of my runs along the river one day, shortly after the reunion, I began to put the pieces together: why not write a book about the lessons those athletes learned through their rowing experiences that helped transform them into successful men? There was not just one but many, many stories of success on this team—in fact, all of them had realized their passions and were playing out their dreams in real life. I wanted to know: Did crew play a part in their success? Did my effort as a coach make an impact? If so, I wanted to share these lessons with others, to help readers learn from these athletes—most of whom had never participated in crew prior to their experience at Dartmouth—how these men became highly successful fathers, professionals, and global leaders.

My life over the past twenty-five years has been filled with opportunities to work with the brightest, most determined, successful businessmen and women. The people who have been the most rewarding to work with have many of the same qualities these oarsmen possessed from the class of '86 freshman crew. I could immediately see parallels in my present-day work with the two different teams of people—oarsmen and business executives—and wanted to learn about how each of these young men had worked their way into leadership positions in their personal and professional lives. Thus, the concept for *Working in Sync* was born.

College Athletes and Success

Is there a parallel between collegiate sports success, lessons learned on the field of play, and success later on in life? According to the *Wall Street Journal*, nearly a third of former student-athletes go on to earn some sort of postgraduate degree. While athletes may have a tendency toward hard work—after all, they worked hard enough to build their skills to get on the team—many college athletes report learning important lessons about hard work, suffering for a goal, victory, and teamwork that they can relate back to as they experience similar situations in their personal and professional lives. These experiences as college athletes extend far beyond the field, river, or arena, and well into their postcollege lives.

What's interesting about this Dartmouth freshman crew is that many of them had never rowed before—and a few of them had never even participated in sports of any kind. So, what is it about crew, in particular, or about the specific experience of that team that helped shape them into the outstanding men they are today? I believe it was a mixture of several factors: the sport itself, as athletes have to work together with precision and strength; the bond they formed, since they were a unique group of personalities; and the unique backgrounds they brought into the Ivy League school.

Understanding the history of crew is important to understanding the concepts in *Working in Sync*. Crew is the oldest intercollegiate sport in this country, and the first event was held in 1852 between Harvard and Yale and rowed on Lake Winnipesaukee in New Hampshire. In this two-mile race, Harvard prevailed over Yale. The Harvard–Yale crew race has been rowed each year since its inception and is now held on the Thames River in New London, Connecticut. Each college has a boathouse on the Thames where the athletes live and train for the race each June. It was here that I saw my first crew race at the age of six.

As I watched that race from high atop the bluff overlooking the Thames with my grandparents, I was full of amazement. I could see two boats slicing through the water far down the river, all the oars entering and leaving the water with such beauty and precision. The bodies of those tall, lean men jumped on each stroke to propel the shell forward. Each boat pushed them to their limit of exhaustion. But it was the beauty of the finish that I remember most clearly: the end of three long, arduous miles of the swing of the oars and the oarsmen working in sync with each other. One group experienced victory; the other, defeat.

As they crossed the finish line that day in June, I was, and still am to this day, taken aback by how much energy the winners have to celebrate and how tired the losers look after defeat. Rowing has been called a "symphony in motion," and each time I watch a race, that thought comes to mind. I was hooked on the sport after watching that first race and have been involved with the sport since I began rowing my freshman year in high school.

The Dartmouth College crew program started in 1933 on Lake Mascoma in New Hampshire about ten miles from the Dartmouth campus. The Dartmouth boathouse is now located just below the campus on the Connecticut River, and the course is one of the favored spots to row for the National and Olympic training teams during the summer months, due to the long stretches of calm river devoid of motor boats, which can cause unwanted wakes. Dartmouth supports a full boathouse of heavyweight, lightweight, and women's teams. In recent years, more than thirty Dartmouth rowers have represented the United States in international competition, including the Pan American Games, World Championships, and Olympic Games.

Dartmouth men's varsity crews have won three Eastern Sprints titles in the past nine years. Rowing is presently the most popular sport at Dartmouth, with over 200 students competing in crew annually.

Those of you who have ventured into the hallways of large corporations have often seen motivational pictures lining the boardroom walls and hallways. Have you ever seen one that represents teamwork? In most cases, it is a wonderful picture of a rowing team taken early in the morning on a beautiful piece of water with water droplets hanging off of the oar blades. But why did they use the rowers to depict the characteristic teamwork? Why not another sport, like baseball, football, lacrosse, or ice hockey? Those activities are all team sports, and nothing should be taken away from the teamwork required to excel in those sports. However, if you have ever had the pleasure of watching a crew race, you have experienced seeing synchronicity in its finest form.

Each athlete in the boat has endured hours of pain and practice. They have dealt with internal voices calling them to stop when pain became too great to continue, yet their teammates were always on their shoulder cheering them on. They had to deal with loss and learn how to be humble as a winner. Crew is one of the ultimate tests of physical strength, endurance, and mental toughness.

Take a moment to look at the cover of this book. Look carefully at the blades. They are all the same height off the water, all going back to the catch at the same time, all "working in sync." They must all go into the water at exactly the same moment, or the shell will be offset to one side, forcing the athletes to adjust their swing and power on the next stroke. The oarsmen, who are unseen in this picture, have practiced for hours and hours to get it just right. They make this boat work as efficiently as they can to bring it up to top speed.

Where do you see this synchronicity happening in your own work environment—where you have a team working together so flawlessly that they know what the others are doing almost without checking in, without looking out of the boat to see where they're going? Do you have the right people in the right seats of the boat in your leadership team?

If just one oar enters the water late, it will throw off the entire swing of the boat. If this error happens over and over, the boat will slow down and could cause a complete stop in movement and momentum. Lack of working in sync leads to continuous defeat and eventually some type of chaos. Is there one person on your team slowing the whole team down? As the leader of your team, what can you do to create an environment of working in sync?

A Process of Insight

While writing *Working in Sync,* I expected to see some obvious connections between lessons learned during crew and success in personal and professional lives many years later. After conducting in-depth interviews with each of the eleven athletes on two different occasions, the book began to take shape. I had the interviews transcribed and then went through the enjoyable task of poring through the information, analyzing each story with close scrutiny and amazement. What came out of these interviews is more than I could have ever predicted, expected, or hoped. I quickly realized that what I'd seen, heard, and experienced at the reunion had to be told. And furthermore, I saw that while all can be considered "successful," each person was so unique in different ways. From high-powered CEOs to outstanding personal triumphs and global accomplishments, each had a compelling story of personal success—one that anyone can relate to and learn from. I know I did. These young men who had once been a team of freshman crew members were now the leaders in their communities, companies, and around the world. I recognized these stories must be told, and my theory that the collegiate sports experience had the potential to create great leaders was unfolding before my eyes. While conducting and rereading the interviews, I started making even more connections to the work I'd done with my executive coaching clients.

Each athlete in this book tells of lessons learned and sacrifices made during their rowing years that they later applied in their work as doctors, entrepreneurs, CFOs, professors, and engineers, among other fields of work. Each chapter has a common theme dealing with such attributes as self-awareness, facing barriers, empathy, and letting others shine, to name a few. These are all areas top executives can benefit from in their own work with their top teams.

Working in Sync connects from the sport of rowing to the inner workings of teams, companies, and organizations—just like the one you lead. When your employees are working in sync, they are working for a common purpose and mission. This is represented in crew by the precision of getting the oars in and out of the water and of pushing beyond limits with reckless abandon to achieve greatness. The spirit of crew is what most leaders desire from their employees, peers, other leaders, and board members. In order for that shell of eight athletes and a coxswain to get down a course to victory, they need to have built trusting relationships and confidence in each other's abilities, suffered through hard, painful work with less than perfect conditions, and trained for long hours without being able to be certain of the results. Yet, there is a reward at the end of the race. Winning is an awesome and very satisfying result for the phenomenal effort. Great teams are not built without superior leadership, or in the case of sports teams, great coaches.

If you have been fortunate enough to have experienced teamwork at the highest levels, you may know the value your experience can bring to the board room, manufacturing floor, or small office environment. Teamwork is not a characteristic that just happens when you put a group of people together, but it is a critical element for companies that want to maximize profitability and neutralize weaknesses. Teamwork takes having knowledge of how to bring people together, along with real-world experience of applying both common sense and strategic principles. *Working in Sync* will give you insights into how eleven oarsmen pursued and created excellence for themselves, their businesses, and their families. These are not merely fables; they are real-life experiences generously shared from the hearts and souls of eleven Dartmouth College student athletes. The hope is to share Ivy League insights along with perspectives from inside a rowing shell to utilize in your workplace and home.

Each chapter contains life-altering lessons, powerful insights, and applicable strategies to transform the way you conduct business, live life, and accomplish goals. Each story is followed by a carefully crafted coaching session—a set of questions, challenges, or thoughts—that can be a powerful part of your personal transformation as you read. My hope is that you get to experience the awe I did as I interviewed each of these former college athletes and then apply the lessons from their lives to enhance your own.

But like anything else, for the eleven amazing stories of *Working in Sync* to have their true impact, you must be willing to invest time and energy into your personal transformation. Are you ready to make the investment in you and your team?

After you've completed this book, challenge yourself to make your own commitment to one of these actions:

1. Pick one of the coaching ideas to practice for the next ninety days.

2. Ask each member of your leadership team to read one chapter each month and have a discussion as one of your monthly professional development initiatives.

Glossary of Crew Terms

Betting shirts: After a race, the T-shirts that are given to the winners by the losers. The betting shirts typically have the rowing emblem from the college of the losing team.

Blade: The piece attached to the end of the oar that enters the water and propels a shell forward.

Bow: The front of the shell and the first part of the boat to cross the finish line.

Coxswain: The person who steers the shell down the course while yelling commands; he's also the ninth person in the boat. The coxswain is responsible for letting the athletes know where the other crews are during the race and is considered the second coach, helping with technical adjustments.

Crew: Members of a rowing team.

Launch: A motorboat that the coach uses to follow along the side of the shell during practice.

Oar: A shaft of wood/graphite with a blade at the end that is used to row a shell. The oar is held at one end by the oarsman, and the end with the blade is placed into the water.

Port: As the coxswain looks down the shell, the port oars are on the left side of the shell.

Riggers: A triangular bracket on a racing shell or other boat to support a projecting oarlock.

Rowing: Moving the boat (shell) through the water.

Seat racing: In order to select the fastest eight oarsmen, the coach will race two shells side by side for short distances, taking the elapsed time for each piece. After a set number of pieces (races), the coach will switch one oarsman from each shell and put them into the other shell. The idea behind seat racing is that the stronger oarsman should make the shell he is in have the fastest time.

Shell: The boat used in crew.

Starboard: As the coxswain looks down the shell, the starboard oars are on the right side of the shell.

Stern: The rear end of the shell and the last part to cross the finish line.

Stroke: A term used to describe an oar going through the water.

Stroke seat: A term that describes the position of the person who sits in the stern of the shell and sets the race pace. He is the eight seat and faces the coxswain.

Throwing the coxswain: The practice of throwing the coxswain into the water after a victory.

Malcolm McIver

Overcoming Adversity
through Faith

About Malcolm

Malcolm McIver is president and part owner of Commerce Properties in Portland, Oregon, a family-owned real estate investment company that works with projects ranging from acquisition to restoration. The owner–manager company boasts 60 years in business and an impressive portfolio of apartment properties and small retail centers. Malcolm constantly adapts his leadership style as the business grows and changes, and he has become an expert at managing a variety of different projects and people.

After graduating from Dartmouth with an AB in economics, Malcolm worked in management consulting in Boston, where he was involved in financial services and organizational restructuring project teams for Fortune 500 companies. While in Boston, he coxed at the National Training Center for the US women's team; he also tried out for the 1988 lightweight national team. But Malcolm's ultimate crew experience was traveling to England after graduation to row in the Henley Royal Regatta. Held in Henley-on-Thames, it is the rowing world's equivalent of Wimbledon and gathers elite rowers from around the world.

In 1991, after completing his MBA at UCLA, Malcolm ventured to Tokyo, Japan, seeking experience in international business. He found a position at Pfizer Pharmaceuticals' headquarters, where he spent the next two-and-a-half years working in pharmaceutical marketing. While his experience in Japan was rewarding, it was also incredibly hard. Used to the space and greenery of Oregon, Tokyo's crowd, pollution, and stress meant he spent much of his three years in Japan depressed. Meeting his wife, Masako Saito, in 1992, gave him a partner who helped him through those difficult times. They married in the spring of 1994 and moved to Portland later that year to join the family business. Malcolm later experienced a life-turning point at a weeklong retreat while supporting his brother, who was overcoming substance abuse challenges. He realized what he needed in life was something beyond himself, a relationship with God.

When Malcolm isn't practicing yoga, coaching basketball, or duck hunting, he enjoys spending time with his family, reading, and building a strong faith life. He and Masako have two daughters, Abby and Bridget.

I See the Buoy

Malcolm had never been in a shell before entering his freshman year at Dartmouth, but he was a natural on the water. As a child, he spent time at his family's lakeside cabin in the Oregon Cascades, where he became comfortable in a canoe, rowboat, sailboat, and motorboat. At the encouragement of a friend from his hometown, along with seeing the shell on the College Green on the Dartmouth campus and being comfortable on the water, Malcolm decided to give college rowing a try. His short stature and lean frame made him a natural choice for the coxswain seat, and although he had no experience in the position, his childhood summers likely contributed to his eventual success in the sport.

The first thing Malcolm noticed about crew was that it was fun… really fun. He enjoyed being in a boat with eight men over six feet tall and weighing in at 180 to 210 pounds, moving down the Connecticut River with such speed, not caring how badly their inexperienced bodies and blades were rowing. He admired his teammates, felt an instant camaraderie with them, and enjoyed the friendships they formed. In fact, he loved everything about the sport.

As the coach of an inexperienced crew, I felt instantly confident in Malcolm's abilities. My sense was that there was a strong confidence that lay behind his quiet demeanor. He would listen intently to my instructions, and I could tell he recognized the importance of his position. I wanted him to know right away that he was my copilot, the extension of the coach on the water. Without a good connection between the coxswain and the coach, the boat speed would suffer, the team would not have the passion for winning, and the "family" would not evolve. He was the key to making this crew go fast, and he took this responsibility early on in training and in races. When he spoke, the team listened. There was never any arrogance or challenge of my coaching decisions—only loyalty and dedication to beating competitors and bringing out the best in his teammates.

The first goal of the season was to beat Yale in our first race. After that, I knew the team would believe in themselves. We needed that win badly, and all of our winter training was focused on that effort. Thankfully, Malcolm bought into that plan. He worked out with the other athletes, which isn't typical of a coxswain. This commitment to sharing the pain contributed to his team pushing harder during practices and again when they hit the water. And his command and control of the boat gave me all the confidence I needed.

The coxswain has numerous roles, all of which create speed. He is the critical link who gets the extra effort during the last twenty strokes from a crew ready to pass out. He is the one who steers a straight course, while keeping his eye on the other crews during a race. He must be aware of the course, buoys, race strategy, distance, and time traveled—all while calculating the finish. He is the connection to the coach. He is the jockey running a one-ton missile down the course with complete abandon. He is the one not counted when people talk about the eight oarsmen; most people forget there are nine people in a shell. Yet he is the one who is celebrated after a victory as he's thrown high in the air, into water that may only be forty degrees in the spring in the Northeast. Throwing the coxswain is a strong tradition after a win, and the class of '86 often tossed Malcolm.

One afternoon, toward the end of a ten-day stay in Tennessee for freshman spring training, the athletes were rowing down the Clinch River, on a nice, long, flat stretch of water in Knoxville. A key part of a coxswain's job is to steer straight to not upset the "set up" of the shell, while also avoiding logs, docks, and any other objects that can damage the shell. The Clinch had numerous navigational buoys meant to guide larger commercial traffic—each four feet tall, made of steel, and easily visible in a regular motorboat—so Malcolm had big targets to watch for during the practices. However, coxswains cannot see what is directly in front of the boat. Their vision is blocked by the rowers' bodies. This is an obstacle to smooth sailing down a river filled with navigational buoys. Malcolm sat alert that day, watching for obstacles. So far, he had shown a sharp eye for buoys and had done an excellent job navigating the boat. Since he was competing for a spot in the first boat, he set out to do an especially good job in the coxswain seat that day.

We were clipping along at three-quarters speed and moving with the current down river. I was off to the side and just behind the boat in the launch, which is a motorboat coaches use to follow alongside the crews as they're rowing. As we came around the final bend, I saw one of those very tall buoys and thought that Malcolm might be steering right for it. After a few moments, I realized Malcolm might not see the giant steel structure the shell and crew were quickly approaching. In those days, when a coach and coxswain needed to communicate, the coach would yell loudly to the coxswain with a megaphone, and the coxswain would respond by raising his hand to acknowledge what the coach said.

I picked up my megaphone and asked, "Malcolm, do you see the buoy?" Malcolm raised his hand in acknowledgment, essentially saying, "I see it, Coach." He continued going straight, directly toward the buoy.

"Malcolm, you see the buoy, right?" I said into the megaphone, my voice growing a little louder. Malcolm raised his hand again but didn't alter the direction of the boat. I wasn't one to doubt Malcolm, so I let the boat continue on, trusting that he'd keep the shell—and team—safe.

We were still rapidly approaching the buoy, which was about 50 yards away at that point, and I began to grow concerned. Megaphone still in my hand and voice more abrupt than before, I shouted, "Malcolm, are you sure you see the buoy?" He raised his hand again, but I could see we were about to crash.

"Weigh enough!" I finally yelled, which means "stop rowing," and the athletes put their oars in the water and dragged them to slow the boat, but it was too late. Suddenly, the buoy looked larger than ever; the bowman's rigger hit hard as the buoy bounced its way down the starboard side, hitting each of the next three riggers. We ended up with a damaged bow rigger and some buoy paint along the hull, but luckily nothing too serious, and there were no injuries except for Malcolm's pride. It took a huge hit. He had seen a buoy but not the one I was questioning.

Two things amazed me about that incident. First, Malcolm was able to move past that event without getting too down on himself. He was understandably embarrassed, but I was surprised to see that he could quickly get his head back into training. When someone is in competition for a seat in the first boat, they want to perform well each time out on the water. But there was something about Malcolm's character, his faith in overcoming difficult situations and mistakes, that helped him accept his error and move on that day in Tennessee.

Not many young men would be able to get back into a boat with confidence after such an egregious error. Second, I realized how much I trusted Malcolm. I trusted him so much, in fact, that I let a boat crash into a buoy! When Malcolm signaled that he saw it, I thought, "If Malcolm says he sees it, he must see it." I had faith in him up until the very last moment. That says a lot about his reliability and confidence level, even at such a young age.

In fact, Malcolm was able to move past that incident with poise and was able to gain a lot from his crew experience. Reflecting on his time with the Dartmouth freshman team, Malcolm says he learned two big lessons. "First, don't worry about the result because that'll always bite you. You won't be able to do your best if you're worried about how things are going to turn out. Second, just focus on giving it your best effort and maximizing your own performance. During that freshman season in 1982, we lost our rhythm and ended up losing to a crew we could have beaten, and I think one of the reasons was that we were preoccupied with winning. We shouldn't have been centered on winning; we should have concentrated on making our boat go as fast as possible. We lost tempo when the other crew jumped out early, and we started thinking, 'Let's not lose!' Our cohesion vanished and the boat slowed down. We rowed well below our top speed, and our worry about losing became self-fulfilling. I am confident to this day the result would have been different if we had focused on performing to our potential and not concerned ourselves so much with being ahead or behind."

He also learned the importance of mentorship and teamwork. He told me years later that I was a great mentor to him and the rest of the guys on the team, a compliment that touched me deeply these many years later. The team also pushed each other, encouraged each other, and cared about each other. They wanted to succeed so that the team would succeed. The positive atmosphere is one Malcolm later worked to create in his workplace and family life, and the lessons he learned during crew—moving past mistakes and being confident in himself—have carried with him, too.

Just like the buoy on the Clinch River, Malcolm has dealt with "buoys" in his life. From learning how to be a better husband and father, to leading his company, to managing his own depression, he's hit some big obstacles. Malcolm believes it's not mistakes or misdirection that's important, but rather how we respond to adversity and allow it to shape our purpose and direction in meaningful ways. Essentially, you must believe you'll become who you're meant to be.

If you ask Malcolm what has gotten him through those trials, he would answer very quickly, "Faith." Throughout his life, God has been an ever-present part of everything he has done, both personally and professionally. "That's what has gotten me through tough times and what has enabled me to get better as a person," Malcolm says. "There's something out there that's greater than I am. I need to be accountable to God, and if I am, if I live in that way, then I really live a joyful and free life."

The second key has been finding groups of good people with whom to share problems and find solutions. Several years ago, he joined a coaching group for CEOs, in which the members share their commitments to bettering their professional and personal lives. Each group is led by a chairperson, an experienced businessperson who coordinates and facilitates group meetings and coaches members individually. The group's sole purpose is to help members gain confidence and clarity in their leadership roles and in what is most important to them in business and life. The fact that Malcolm was exposed to coaching and teamwork in crew likely made this team approach appealing in his executive role. The members of the group, all of whom have similar challenges, have helped Malcolm find balance in his personal and professional life, while enhancing the perspective of *others first*, which he carries into his day-to-day work.

As much as he personally strives to become who he's meant to be, Malcolm's main focus as a leader is getting the best out of his team. His goal is to help it grow into its fullest potential at his company, and to do so, he focuses on three main actions:

1. Accountability
2. Treating people with dignity
3. Goal setting

Holding people accountable is something he has developed over the years; by his own admission, he wasn't great at it back in his crew days. He realized that he could have done a better job demanding performance from his teammates, and when he became CEO of the family business, he focused on learning how to hold people accountable, both by recognizing achievements and addressing shortcomings. Through coaching and mentoring, Malcolm recognized and dealt with his blind spots, areas in which he wasn't able to see his own shortcomings. He was also able to finally deal decisively with his depression, conquering it with help from others. Having someone hold him accountable for those areas has been hugely important for him, and he does the same for his work team. Malcolm says, "If you don't have a conversation about shortcomings, you'll never get to the result, so it's worth going through the discomfort of talking about the things you usually avoid discussing. If you can help people grow in a way that's going to let them get past some of their own roadblocks or fulfill their own potential, then it's worth it."

Throwing the Coxswain

After every win, the coxswain welcomes the inevitable: getting tossed into the frigid waters of the rowing venue. In the case of the class of '86, that meant it was Malcolm. It didn't matter the temperature of the air or water—after the team won a race, they would pick Malcolm up by his hands, feet, or whatever else they could grab, lift him above their heads, and toss him as high as they could into the water, turning and spinning him in the air. This tradition carried throughout the whole season...and Malcolm's entire time in crew.

In addition to accountability, Malcolm feels treating people with dignity and providing the tools they need to succeed is critical. He's very clear about expectations and encourages individuals to ask for help or guidance to gain these tools. Although he used to get frustrated when people weren't performing at the levels he wanted them to, he learned the value of patience and respect. As he explains, everyone has a different way of communicating and processing information, and it won't do any good to become upset if someone doesn't "get it." Taking the time to slow down, understand another person's viewpoint, and communicate in such a way that the person listens to you pays big dividends in performance and workplace satisfaction. Patience is a characteristic often overlooked but one that's become essential to Malcolm over the years.

While Malcolm's leadership strategies have been an important part of his success, faith remains the most important aspect. "What has helped me the most is knowing everybody I deal with is made in the image of God, and everyone has a holy aspect," he says. This perspective helps him focus on the good in people, rather than getting angry when adversity strikes. Once, a tenant negotiated in bad faith and didn't follow through with an agreement, which ended up costing Malcolm's company a lot of money. Although it was a big hit, he decided to let go of his anger and move past the situation. Remembering the tenant was made in the image of God helped Malcolm approach the eventual legal settlement without bitterness. Constantly remaining aware of the inherent divinity in others underpins all his growth as a leader.

Malcolm's heart for others sets him apart, and his desire to help employees grow and succeed makes him a great leader. His belief in God helps him see others with a different perspective, even when they act in bad faith. And the wonderful people who surround him have made him into the man he is today—a great husband, father, leader, and teammate.

Ask Questions

"Asking questions is a very powerful way to lead," Malcolm explains. "Rather than telling people what they should be doing, ask them a lot of questions, without a specific end result in mind. They can't be questions that are just rhetorical. Rather, ask a lot of open-ended questions to help people think things through on their own and reach conclusions. As a leader, you still have veto power over the conclusion, but the idea is to help them think through things so they can develop and focus on that process—that problem-solving skill—and develop their own action and leadership skills."

Whit's Words

What are the barriers or buoys in your life right now? How you deal with adversity will be instrumental in how you live your life. All of us have had disappointments, failures, misgivings, and tragedies during our time on this earth; others deal with smaller things that are big obstacles in their work or personal lives. Malcolm was able to find the courage and the strength to recognize something was adrift in his life and turn to his faith to help him deal with his own internal battles.

Whether you're dealing with great pain or trying to navigate a smaller buoy, know that when you reach out to others, you are not a burden. Don't deny others the joy of helping you. It takes courage to admit and seek counsel, but know you will impact others by taking that first step.

Write your answers to these questions in Step 1, and then find a partner, colleague, peer, or friend, and follow the directions in Step 2.

Step 1: Identify Barriers

1. What are the barriers/buoys in your life today?

2. What have you tried to do in the past to move past these barriers?

3. How did it work?

4. What do you need to do differently?

5. What will you do differently?*

---

*Steve Morris, *Leadership Simple: Leading People to Lead Themselves* (Santa Barbara, CA: Imporex International, Inc., 2003).

Step 2: Accountability/Responsibility

1. Now that you have a partner, peer, or colleague invested in your success, agree on a timetable for regular check-ins. Create self-accountability measures so your peer coach knows what your expectations are for change. This will give him/her concrete metrics to help you achieve your desired goal(s) for overcoming those barriers.

2. It's best to set up short weekly meetings so too much time doesn't pass once you decide on your commitments. Have a clear agenda with outcomes for your meetings.

You might find that your partner also wants to discuss an issue/barrier that is impeding their progress in one area of their life. Be available and supportive, if that's the case. It's amazing that when others see success, they, too, may want to improve in some area of their own lives.

If you are having trouble identifying barriers in your life but know something just isn't right, you might want to try the following:

1. Draw a big circle on a piece of paper and divide it into eight sections, like a pie. Write in these eight different aspects of your life into one of the slices: (1) work, (2) health, (3) spiritual, (4) financial, (5) love life, (6) environment, (7) friends and family, and (8) professional development.

2. Rate the degree of satisfaction in your life in each of the slices. On a scale of 1 to 10, how satisfied are you with each faction of your life?

3. Look over your ratings and decide which area needs some attention. For example, you may discover that if you improve your health, other areas will also improve.

4. For the areas you want to change, decide what you want to "Start Doing" and what you want to "Stop Doing." Create a timetable for your committed actions.

5. Go back every three months and rate each area again to see what has changed. Did you find some new barriers that have prevented you from living your ideal life? If so, go back to Step 1 to see what to do.

There is more and more research coming out that shows that people are more motivated to change based on their pain than on the gain of rewards associated with change. Ask yourself, what are the consequences short and long term if you don't make any changes? What are the rewards for making change? Is the pain great enough to create change and is the benefit great enough to sustain change?

Reflecting back at your past, how have you dealt with barriers and pain? You can be reactive or proactive. Will you ignore the pain and hope it goes away or, like Malcolm who turned to his faith, will you create a strategy that eliminates those barriers that are getting in the way of living the life you deserve?

Hans Stander

*Empowering People and Building
Countries through Storytelling*

About Hans

Hans Stander built private equity investment programs focused on China, Taiwan, India, Brazil, Russia, and most recently, sub-Saharan Africa. Through his work in these markets and with smaller projects in other countries, an estimated one million people have gotten jobs as a result of the capital he helped deploy. In 2009, he became a partner at Surya Capital Management, LP, a company that focuses on private equity in Africa. There, he coleads pipeline development, human capital recruitment, investor cultivation, and relationship management.

As a young man, he worked at the US State Department, the White House, and with the CEO of Pillsbury's subsidiary in Venezuela. In addition to receiving the Rintels Prize and the Rockefeller Memorial Prize, he was awarded Rockefeller Foundation and Coro Foundation fellowships, which eventually led him to Harvard's Kennedy School of Government and subsequently the Business School. He graduated from Harvard with his MA in public policy and cum laude with a BA in government from Dartmouth.

Hans calls the birth of each of his six children his most memorable highlights in his life and pronounces his wife, Johanna von Stauffenberg, a saint. He engages his children in nightly stories crafted from his creative imagination, a quality he has mastered and used extensively to convince his clients to invest in some of the poorest countries in the world.

Hans lives with Johanna and his kids—Ferdinand, Damian, Griffin, Marie, Anna, and Heinrich—primarily in Risstissen, Germany. In his free time, he enjoys tennis, sailing, horseback riding, and the travel that is inevitable with his work.

Big Dreams and Engaging Stories

How is it that some people have the gift of "dreaming big"? These individuals are able to see practical ways of achieving what others would call impossible. Hans Stander is one such individual—a person who has never shied away from the extraordinary and has no trouble envisioning himself and others doing great things.

During his childhood, Hans went to an all-boys prep school in Kansas City, Missouri. With his father as the headmaster and his mother an art teacher, he spent most of his youth under close supervision and scrutiny. Although he excelled academically and athletically, he explored the person he wanted to become within a conservative community. When he arrived at Dartmouth his freshman year and joined the soccer team, the new liberty and freedom brought some unexpected challenges—especially when it came to making good decisions in his social life. His soccer coach noticed his behavior getting out of hand and pulled him aside one day. "Hans," his coach told him, "I think you need to take a break from sports and decide what is truly important to you."

Hans was shocked and crushed. Sports were an important part of his life, and he hadn't realized his lifestyle choices were going to affect what mattered most to him. Over the next few days, he thought long and hard about what he could do to impose structure into his life. And then it hit him: join the rowing team. He knew crew was a sport that required intense dedication, unmatched time commitment, and a level of discipline no other sport on campus demanded. Plus, he was a swimmer, which is a great addition to any crew, since swimmers understand pain, monotony, and water! He felt crew would force structure into his life, and so he tried out for the team.

One Million Jobs

"After my first decade-and-a-half of work in private equity for emerging market companies, one of the limited partners spoke with me about a research project she had completed and told me she had done calculations based on decade-long growth and results from the investment program in all of those markets," Hans reflects. *"She calculated over a million people had gotten jobs, directly and indirectly, in those markets as a consequence of the capital I had helped deploy.*

"For me, that's one of the accomplishments I really feel great about. In many markets like India, Africa, or China, there are hundreds of millions of incredibly poor people. Creating a financial future for people in those countries involves foresight into some kind of stability, which eventually allows them to put their kids in school, pay for hospital care they otherwise never would have been able to afford, and maybe even get a mortgage and buy a house."

Hans soon found crew offered much more than he'd expected. He learned to push beyond what he thought were his limits—a foundational principle that served him later in life. "On several different occasions in my freshman year, Whit's style of encouragement set the foundation for me as a people builder," Hans says. "I remember being in the gym during winter workouts, and we had been running around the track doing sprints. We were just completely exhausted, totally knackered. Then, we had to do weight circuit training, and I had to do bench pulls, where you pull the barbell up to your chest as you're laying prone on a bench. I got to twenty-one reps shy of the one minute cut-off, and I just didn't think I could go any further. All of a sudden, Coach was in my ear. He said, 'Hans, come on, you can do it. I believe in you,' and sure enough, I squeezed out four more. I think that commitment to push beyond the boundary of what you think is your limit is an extraordinary achievement from what might be considered average. And a great coach helps you discover the limits that extend beyond those you can reach on your own."

Hans was struck by what the team was able to achieve together. Looking at the sizes, body compositions, and weights of all the people on the Dartmouth freshman team, it was easy to see they couldn't physically compare with the highly athletic teams they went up against, most of whom were basically a uniform six feet three inches. But although the Dartmouth athletes had ups and downs in training, they finally achieved that perfect swing where it felt like they were flying on the water. As Hans puts it, my coaching skills finally got them all rowing in sync.

Hans also learned to build others up, to make sure that his actions didn't negatively impact those around him, even unintentionally. The team regularly would run grueling hill sprints, and although the training was hard work, Hans usually finished strong, a few strides ahead of the next athlete. At that time, his style was very self-deprecating. One day, after he finished first in an especially difficult running drill, Hans complained, "Oh, my God, that was so hard!" He acted depleted, as though his body were going to give way underneath him. But the team had to do the drill again, and he finished first that time, too, and made the same complaints.

Hans recalls: "I didn't realize the impact that had on my teammates until Whit came up to me and said, 'Hans, how do you think it makes the others feel when you continually beat everyone and then complain about how hard the work is? One of your teammates came up to me and said that you were actually demotivating him. You're always finishing two or three strides ahead of him, but then you complain as though you're about to collapse and disintegrate. What you want to try to do is inspire him.' "

When I said this, the "light-bulb moment" happened and Hans looked at me with sincere appreciation for the epiphany. He'd never considered that his actions—actions he wasn't really even aware of— affected his teammates in such a big way. From that point on, he chose his words wisely to inspire those around him. He knew it didn't have to be blatant or over-the-top—he could *literally* lead by example.

Perhaps what affected Hans the most in crew was the idea of dreaming big and aiming for a goal. "Crew is about setting an audacious goal, and then harnessing people's skills to work in synchronicity toward achieving that goal," he reflects. "I think that has influenced almost everything I've done since the days of crew."

Of course, Hans's story didn't stop with crew—in fact, it was just a start to the fantastic journey of his life. After freshman year, he took some time off to work in the State Department on Latin American economic development policy. One evening, he was at a party at a family friend's house in Georgetown. There was an old cider press being used to crank out fresh cider. He saw an older gentleman putting apples into the press and cranking the wheel to squeeze the apple juice into the cider vat. The man seemed to be having difficulty with the crank, so Hans walked over and asked if he could give him a hand. It turned out the gentleman was the former head of the State Department's legal department, and Hans ended up talking with him for several hours. Finally, the man said, "It sounds like you're peaking in terms of your learning curve with the State Department. Why don't you let me set up an interview for you?"

The interview was with Ronald Reagan's head lawyer, Boyden Gray, and Hans was offered a job. Within weeks, he had moved from Foggy Bottom to the Old Executive Office Building. Subsequently, he worked with the CEO of Pillsbury's subsidiary in Latin America, where he learned about accelerating economic development in a less advantaged part of the world. His experience there would shape the course of his career, although he wasn't completely aware of it at the time. Of course, this opportunity put a big break in his college and crew experience because he ended up staying there for about nine months and came back to school in the off-season.

Be a First Settler

Hans remembers being in a board of directors meeting with Henry Kissinger, who often had an influential voice as to whether projects would go forward. Hans will never forget his words: "Hans, you must always remember it's better to be a first settler than a pioneer."

Hans eventually returned to Dartmouth to finish his education. At graduation, Hans was honored with several awards and asked to publish his senior thesis, which led to fellowships from the Rockefeller Foundation and the Coro Foundation, and eventually to Harvard for graduate school. But after completing his master's degree in public policy, he decided that his original plan—getting a PhD at Harvard—wasn't the right fit. His drive to work in emerging markets led him to drop out and join Credit Suisse First Boston's global privatization group; there, he worked with Bayo Ogunlesi and many others on projects in the United States and all over the world, including China, Latin America, and Europe. From the educational and real-life work

experience, he concluded the private sector had an extremely important role to play in accelerating growth in less developed parts of the
world. But after four years, Hans decided the transactional side wasn't
motivating to him. He was a builder, and he wanted to work in private
equity, where a team manages third-party capital to invest in private
companies and subsequently builds those businesses into segment
leaders in their markets.

Hans joined an asset management company in Los Angeles in
early 1995 called Trust Company of the West. There, he helped found
and build one of the first emerging market, private equity franchises.
The first business was set up in China, then in Taiwan, India, Brazil,
Mexico, Argentina, and Russia. In each case, his job was to decide
which markets to go after and then define the strategy, recruit the
team, and help raise the capital. Trying to raise the first private equity
fund in the world for India in 1996 was considered virtually impossible. When Hans set his sights on Africa in 2009 and 2010, the entire
financial fabric of the world felt like it was going to implode. Trying to
convince people investing in Africa was a good thing—not only would
they get a good return, but the social impact of their investments would
further leverage financial return—was considered challenging, at best.
Each one of those times, Hans knew most people saw his plans as high
risk from a career perspective.

But Hans has never been afraid of setting very risky goals for
himself. He learned how through difficult training, while completing
twenty-mile rows on the Connecticut River. In the most trying of
races, when you really think you cannot go that extra kilometer or
make that last leg of the race, in fact, you can reach down, you can
dig down deeper, and you can find an incredible reserve of energy
and power. This reserve can carry you not only beyond the finish line
but farther than you might otherwise have thought possible.

"Crew really taught me, in a lot of ways, how to align internal and external stakeholders toward a common shared vision," Hans says. "When you are doing something extraordinary in a company, organization, or—in the case of my team and me, in entire countries, such as China, India, and Ethiopia—you have to build confidence, vision, and inspiration for the task at hand with potential private investors and the leaders who will carry out the work. With these audacious goals, you have to put a strategy together to make it tangible and then repeatable. The skills I have developed are empowering skills, which enable people to realize their full potential through a shared common purpose. Crew training and racing set the standard to teach me you had better be ready to tackle what most say is impossible if you are going to achieve anything really new and unique in the global world of business."

Real-World Experience Matters

Nothing beats the crucible of experience if you are alert, aware, and responsive to those you want to harness to your cause.

Of course, Hans can't do all this good on his own. He has to draw together talented team members, guiding and inspiring them. "When younger people join our firm, I try to define a canvas upon which they can paint, but with clear borders and guidelines. The canvas has a frame, and the type of painting is defined, but they know what brushes, what colors, what style is used. I'm supportive of experimentation, and that sometimes results in some false starts, but I think, in the long run, it builds resilient teams who are capable of calling on capabilities within themselves and have more control over the momentum of the snowball."

Perhaps the most important strategy Hans practices in his professional life is to alleviate fear through storytelling. When he works with people in developing countries, their fears are even more pervasive than most people in the United States would understand. "Fear immobilizes and restrains action; it prevents risk-taking," Hans says. "It is sand in the wheels of progress, because great leaps in human progress throughout history really happen only through the insane pursuits of people defying all those around who are saying, 'That is impossible. You are such a dreamer; come back to reality.' Eliminating the perceptions of risk is critical to help people see what is accurate and factual. What I do is empower individuals with the belief in what is possible, the knowledge, the experience, and the tools to see more clearly the opportunity but also the authentic risks, so decisions can be made based on unsentimental facts." He does this through telling compelling stories built on foundations of fact that reach his audience at the most fundamental level. And he has gotten good at this skill just like in crew: practice, practice, practice. He tests, refines, tests again, and refines anew until he gets to something that is repeatable and works with extreme effectiveness.

Investing in Your Children

Hans doesn't just dream big for people in other countries— he starts at home. "My biggest hope is for my kids to find an exciting world of hope, which continues to grow, and that they continue building up their confidence and their abilities to define a path that is enriching for them," he says.

In 2012, Hans's organization launched an effort to bring infra-structure funding to Ethiopia, one of the poorest countries in the world per capita. Despite the obvious obstacles, Hans firmly believes in the story of Ethiopia—that the Ethiopian people are no different than other people in the world, and they can change the course of history by bringing economic growth to the region. Hans can't accomplish this alone, so he'll do what he does best: inspire others by making big dreams palpable and real. He'll tell the story and build the vision, encourage others to join him in making audacious goals a reality— and change lives in the process.

Whit's Words

Hans has mastered two areas of communication that have created phenomenal results in his ability to raise capital for some of the poorest nations in the world: presenting and storytelling.

Excellence in persuasion and leadership starts with listening and understanding the needs, aspirations, fears, and constraints of an audience, a community, or a team, and then tailoring your pitch to fit with their beliefs and values. Obviously, the more authentic and legitimate the fit, the more likely one is to align interests and achieve a common purpose. I asked Hans to share some "words of wisdom" for others who need to master the skills of presenting and storytelling. Immediately following his insights, I have included questions and strategies to complement his words.

You must help people find meaning in the common purpose you are communicating, something to believe in and aspire to beyond the paycheck, bonus, or return on investment. Certainly, commercial success is a must, and the logic and rigor of any analysis or pitch must stand on its own, but the world in which we live in today, by nature, atomizes, fragments, and disintegrates. People yearn for a sense of meaning, a sense of purpose that transcends the "job" or "project." Thinking through and articulating what that purpose could be may feel "fluffy," but when it finds its audience, it ensures commitment.

Small goals, small dreams, don't have the power to ignite people to make the leap from thought to feeling. Only big ideas have the power to align people's hearts with their heads. And when that is achieved, great achievements are possible because "intellectual and emotional conviction" combine to sustain the effort through inevitable valleys, which must be traversed to reach the peaks. So, make the linkages clear and understandable between the commercial aims and the larger, more laudable purpose that is built on the shared values and beliefs of the team or community.

So often, we spend our time explaining the what, where, who, and how of a business plan. Explaining the "why" is where it should all start. And that "why" needs to be about more than simply making money. Practice the business plan pitch or whatever stories you are presenting and test the audience's reaction. Listen carefully to that reaction and then refine your pitch. And repeat the cycle until more yes answers than noes result. Simply the experience and learning that result can teach these skills.

When creating your own message, consider these questions:

- What is your point of view? It is not important that they agree with you, but they should be clear about where you stand!

- How do you really feel about your subject? The audience has to feel your passion as they listen. If you're passionate about your message, it will come out with emotions and believability. When you get this right, you're going to change lives, beliefs, and attitudes.

- What are their needs and interests? What do they know about the subject you're going to deliver to them? Know the demographics of your audience.

- What do you want them to leave with? Think about the benefits your audience will gain from hearing you speak.

- What action steps do you hope they will take back to work with them based on your presentation? Give them three tips that they can apply once they return to work without the need to contact you.

Once you have answered these questions, you're ready to put together the body of your presentation:

1. Start with a story, some humor, an analogy, a quote, or some visual pictures to get the audience engaged in you and what you are saying.

2. State the benefits you have enjoyed from your area of expertise. What might the benefits be for your audience?

3. Announce three key points you're going to cover during your presentation. People can remember three key points. Use your talents in storytelling to draw them into your conversation.

4. In your summary, review your key points and challenge them to take one of the key points to practice back at work or at home. Close with a story that captures the essence of your point of view.

As Hans said, once you have your presentation put together, you need to practice it so you can get more "*yes* answers than *noes*." Then, you know you've mastered storytelling and presenting.

Garth T. Mark

*Respect for People through
Personal Integrity*

About Garth

Garth T. Mark is a catering and events coordinator for a global, 400-employee ad agency in New York City. His role involves planning meals for the company's biggest clients and special out-of-office events, as well as stocking and maintaining the agency's seven kitchens. Essentially a one-man show, Garth balances a heavy workload that requires top-level industry expertise and excellent management and organizational skills.

In 1993, he formed a partnership with three other people to open one of New York City's first boutique espresso bars, bringing the Northwest coffee experience to the Big Apple. The venture was an incredible financial success, and he helped launch the personalized coffee experience in the city, resulting in many similar establishments opening their doors. In addition to this endeavor, he spent twelve years as an actor in New York City, working in the theater and making appearances in TV shows, including "Law and Order," and also cooked in restaurants in Vail, Seattle, Chicago, and New York.

Today, Garth lives in Fort Greene, Brooklyn, where he spends almost every Saturday at the Greenmarket, buying locally grown food for the week. He is active in the Appalachian Mountain Club, and he takes at least one trip a year in the western United States river rafting and hiking.

More than Money

Garth T. Mark was fourteen when he saw his first crew race on television. As he watched that Oxford–Cambridge race, he thought rowing looked like a sport he'd like to compete in someday. When he got a little older and started applying for colleges, he made sure that each school had a crew. When he was admitted to Dartmouth

College, he was excited to try something new but worried he wouldn't have the skill level to qualify for the first boat. After all, he assumed many of the freshmen had attended prep school and had probably been rowing for three or four years already. Luckily, that wasn't the case with most of the crew athletes in the class of '86.

During his first days on campus, Garth was walking along and saw a shell sitting on the Dartmouth Green. Intrigued, he made his way over and met the guys who were out recruiting for crew. Each was welcoming and encouraging, and Garth quickly realized many of the rowers had come from diverse athletic backgrounds and that rowing would be a great opportunity for growth. As he stood there, taking in the fall colors, the clear sky, and the kind welcome he'd received, he thought, "This is a good way to start my four years."

Like many of the young athletes on the Dartmouth freshman '82 crew, Garth quickly learned that crew wasn't just about mastering technique and learning to glide swiftly and gracefully across the water. In fact, it was a lot of work—and a lot of fun. Although he'd been a high school athlete, the concepts of active recovery and cross-training were completely new to him. "There were things about Whit's coaching that were very different from any experience I'd had in high school," Garth says. "He introduced me to the whole concept of active recovery, which I had never heard of before—essentially, cross-training and making practice fun and different each day, as opposed to just hard, laborious workouts. I always looked forward to what was going to be different about practice. While I knew we were going to spend tons of time on the indoor rowing ergometers, I also knew there was going to be something else, something to be learned. I have continued cross-training since then—biking, swimming, kayaking. I really mix it up, and it makes a huge difference in the longevity of my training."

For Garth, the fun didn't stop on the water or during practice—it extended to the dinner table. Inspired by two Italian uncles who loved to eat well,and having spent the previous summer cooking in a restaurant on the Puget Sound, it wasn't surprising that Garth also became the "team cook." Each week, he organized a pasta dinner for the guys, and this became a ritual they looked forward to, a time when they could kick back and enjoy each other's company.

Crew wasn't always so enjoyable. One of the first practices for spring training took place on a frigid morning, and the bitter cold weather was only amplified by being on the water. Getting out on the river in early March, the temperature a bone-chilling 33 degrees, in the sleeting rain and icy winds, made for a quick wake-up call. Once the river opens up from the winter ice, the water runs fast. Even though the ice had broken apart to open up the river, the icebergs continued to flow south from Canada for a number of weeks, daily damaging the underside of the rowing shells. That morning, large pieces of ice were running by the docks as the team put the boat into the water at 6:00 a.m.

As Garth rowed along with his teammates, the icy air felt like it was seeping into his bones. Those first ten minutes warming up, Garth could feel the effects of the weather against his body as the wind and rough water hit the riggers, sending frozen icicles into his back. The memory of his warm dorm room and comfort of deep sleep were long gone as he made his way down the river. "I remember looking at my hands, frozen like claws around the oar, and I didn't think I could make the row. I was having illusions about amputation, but I knew that wasn't going to happen, and I couldn't let the fear take over. Then, I heard Whit urging us onward from the launch. That helped me push forward. If I didn't have someone supporting me in my time of doubt, I think it would have been impossible to keep going."

That row wasn't an isolated event—there were many other times during practice when Garth felt he'd reached the end of his abilities as an athlete. But he learned that he needed to give his all while in the boat, and he couldn't leave any part of his energy and effort untapped. He also found the value in teamwork, in pushing alongside the other athletes and collectively finding the strength to carry on in the most grueling and trying conditions. He had a strong sense of respect for his teammates, as they did for him. "The interesting thing about rowing," he remarks, "is that you're really in your own world in many ways, but you're also part of a much larger entity." The idea of being a part of something—of each member contributing to the essence of the whole, each person bringing value to the endeavor—carried with him well beyond crew, as far as New York City.

In 1993, Garth was living in Seattle. The Seattle of the '90s was very much like it is today—every block had a coffee shop; there were coffee carts on every corner, and ordering a morning espresso drink was a personalized experience. Regulars could walk into shops and baristas would recognize them and start their orders before they even paid for their drinks. The approach was a customized, community-oriented one. But in New York City at the time, such places didn't exist. Coffee giants like Starbucks hadn't yet entered the espresso market either, so there weren't chain options for coffee lovers. Most people in New York City associated espresso drinks with Little Italy or the West Village, bought drip coffee from a diner or a bodega, or got espresso from a machine—there wasn't the daily, personal experience of buying a cup of joe. Garth saw an incredible opportunity to bring the Pacific Northwest-style experience to the Big Apple and joined with three other entrepreneurs to make his vision a reality. He knew it would be a success.

Know Your Business

"If you're running a business, it makes a huge difference if you know the business from the ground up," Garth says. "I know a lot of people somehow become professional managers, and they feel they could manage any business because they have managerial principles. But unless you know your business inside-out, you're at a loss. You'll never really get it 100 percent."

As the only one of the four who had kitchen experience, Garth's job was to keep the place running while creating a great customer experience. He hadn't invested capital up front, so his share was earned through sweat equity—and he certainly earned his percentage of the business, working six days a week, twelve to fourteen hours a day. Pushing past fatigue and exhaustion during crew served him well as he got through those long, grueling days. Although he began to see problems from the start, he felt that if he did his job well and ran the shop smoothly, everyone would be happy.

Like Garth predicted, the venture was wildly successful. "We made a lot of money at a time when rent in New York City was affordable," Garth explains. "My partners were interested in making money fast— they wanted to open the requisite number of shops, then begin franchising. And they were willing to sacrifice quality to get there. I wanted to build The Temple of Coffee. Soon I thought to myself, 'This is not the way to do business and build a reputation.' Through a lot of things I saw them do, especially the money that was being thrown around, I knew I just didn't want to emulate that. That's not what I wanted for my future, especially in New York."

As Garth stepped back and looked at the greed that had seemed to take over his partners, he knew he'd have to step out of the venture after his one-year commitment. Some of his core values were being tested, and he wasn't willing to sacrifice his integrity to make money. From the start, he'd insisted on fair wages for employees, hoping to attract and retain talented baristas and wait staff, but his partners felt people were disposable and easily replaced. Along with caring for those in his charge, Garth knew that forming a business identity would be nearly impossible with high turnover, but the other three investors couldn't see this. His partners were so driven by money and success, they failed to recognize that the most fundamental part of any business is the people who run it.

Treat Customers Like Royalty

"Customers expect quality at a competitive price," Garth says. "The highest expectation the customer has is to be treated like royalty. If they are not treated royally, they will fire you and find another company who will treat them properly."

Eventually, two of the partners moved on, so it was just Garth and the principal investor left. To put it mildly, these two didn't see eye to eye. Each had a different vision for the place. Garth wanted to create a shop that offered a personalized customer experience, treated employees and vendors well, and functioned with the utmost honesty and integrity, while his partner only saw dollar signs. At the one-year mark, Garth stepped away from that venture. He'd had the success many dream of in one of the most exciting cities in the world, had introduced an entire new concept to one of the most innovative places on the planet, and he'd done it all without sacrificing who he was or his beliefs.

The espresso bar venture taught Garth a great deal about how *not* to act as a business owner—and how to learn from failure. "I think breaking new ground is really important," Garth explains. "You have to challenge yourself. And something I've discovered that I didn't really know before is you have to fail. You have to fall on your face a few times, and you just learn so much more from that than from succeeding." He saw that a person could be successful doing the wrong things while not treating people well, but he didn't want to be that way.

There are a couple of other lessons he carries with him today, one learned as a chef at a high-end restaurant and another as an actor, both in New York City.

One evening, Garth was cooking at a restaurant with a very high-priced menu. As he made his dishes, he noticed the cook next to him was throwing expensive ingredients together, not taking pride in his work. The sous-chef came over, saw what Garth's coworker was doing, and said, "Look, these people come here with expectations. They're getting dressed up, they have made reservations, it's a special night for them, and they're paying a lot of money. You know not everyone who comes into this restaurant is wealthy. This may just be a one-time thing for them. Take some pride!" As Garth listened, he came to a realization that would fuel his business philosophy forever: everyone is a VIP. The status of VIP doesn't just apply to the wealthiest of the wealthy. Whether a client is rich or enjoying a special experience, that person deserves to be treated with respect and care.

Aside from food, one of Garth's greatest interests was acting. During an acting class one day, his teacher said to him, "Every time you get on stage, you're going to have to leave a piece of yourself up there, and you have to believe in yourself to do that. You're on the stage a lot, so you have to leave a piece of yourself wherever you go."

In his day-to-day activities, Garth carries that sense of conviction into everything he does. He gives 100 percent of himself and leaves a percentage behind, knowing that—like in crew—he'll somehow find a way to build it back up, to push beyond what he thought were his limits. "You have to have faith in yourself that you have enough in you to do that," he says. "And if you're not in an organization where you have that kind of support, which allows you to give of yourself, I don't think you'll ever get the result you're seeking."

Garth's plans for the future are in sync with his commitment to people and the community. "There's a whole local-grown movement, where people use all local produce in their restaurants. I would like to have a place with my own hydroponic garden, so I could grow produce year-round. I'd like to do something to stimulate the economy wherever I end up living. I really miss being closer to the production of food, and I want to get the experience of working directly with farmers to get the top produce and showcase it in a way that would make them proud." Whatever he does in the future, it's sure to be done with integrity, drive, and a people-focused approach.

Set Your Own Standards

"A lot of the younger people who are coming into organizations are constantly trying to impress their superiors," Garth comments. "But if you're only interested in impressing those people above you, and you forget about the people around you or under you, you may rise through the hierarchy, but you're never really going to set your own standards. You'll never break new ground."

Whit's Words

How do you instill great customer integrity, honesty, respect, and loyalty, into upcoming younger leaders, who may feel success is all about impressing the manager, VP, or CEO? Garth knew all along that his high standards of integrity would lead to the great results he achieved as he began his entrepreneurial espresso business in New York City. He made some tough life choices based on the fact that integrity was being violated in his partnerships. Instead of continuing down the path of greed, poor service, and low standards, he chose to follow his internal compass, delivering high-quality products to loyal customers.

Today, there are hundreds of espresso bars and corner coffee cafés all competing with giants like Starbucks. What do you love about your coffee shop, whether it's the local hangout or a big chain? How could you transfer those feelings and experiences into your own organization? Is your product really different enough to drive customers to your door?

Customer service is a concept in many businesses but not always a reality. Many people don't grow up with the idea that every person should be treated like a VIP. So, how do you teach the idea of great service and respect for all?

The keys to treating customers as VIPs are to ask, listen, and observe. It is counterproductive to assume we know what our customers want or need. Instead, we need to find appropriate ways to ask. The Kano Model of Quality (one of the fundamental modes used in Total Quality Management) provides some great ideas to explore three levels of customer engagement (or disengagement).

The first level of customer needs involves the minimums or absolutes in order to do business together. We can discover these by paying close attention to complaints and asking customers who don't do business with us, or quit doing business with us, why we have failed to win their business.

The second level of customer needs can be described as "more is better." These are the benefits they receive that cause them to do business with us instead of someone else. Key questions to identify these needs are:

- How are we doing?
- How can we do better?
- Why do you choose to do business with us?

The third level of customer needs can be described as "delighters," the true emergence of VIP treatment that creates raving fans. These are new ideas, products, and services we provide that surprise our customers in ways that are useful. When we create the solution before they know they need it, they are surprised and can't help bragging about what we have done for them.

True VIP service pays attention to all three levels and periodically solicits feedback, while recognizing every customer's needs are dynamic and evolving over time. A "more is better" or "delighter" customer benefit today can quickly become an absolute necessity tomorrow.

Scott Sandell

Letting Others Shine
Leads to Superior Results

Scott Sandell

About Scott

Scott Sandell is a general partner at New Enterprise Associates (NEA), one of the top five venture capital firms in the world, according to *Forbes Magazine*. NEA has $13.5 billion under management. Scott heads the technology investing practice, which is about 70 percent of NEA's investment activity. Since joining the firm in 1996, he has personally led investments in industry-transforming companies, including Salesforce.com, Data Domain, Workday, and Fusion I/O. He's also been on the Forbes Midas List of top tech investors numerous times and was recently named chairman-elect of the National Venture Capital Association. Along with serving as lead director for two public companies, he sits on the boards of ten others, has successfully completed public offerings or mergers for sixteen companies, and is constantly looking for the next big venture.

Before joining NEA, Scott worked at Microsoft, where he was involved in developing Windows 95. He began his career at the Boston Consulting Group and also worked as a salesperson for C-ATS Software, where he founded and ran the company's European subsidiary. He has an MBA from Stanford and graduated from Dartmouth College with a BA in engineering sciences.

Scott grew up in a small town in Connecticut but now lives in Northern California with his wife, whom he met at Stanford, and their three children. He considers meeting his wife one of the highlights of his life. In his free time, Scott enjoys the great outdoors through mountain biking, backpacking, fly fishing, and rafting, and takes pleasure in cooking and photography.

Giving Back at Henley

The moment Scott saw Dartmouth, he fell in love with it. During Scott's sophomore year in high school, his father spent six months on sabbatical at the Cold Regions Research and Engineering Laboratory (CRELL), located a couple of miles north of Hanover. Every other weekend, Scott's mother would drive up to Hanover with Scott and his brother and sister. That was young Scott's first exposure to campus. As it would turn out, he would have his pick of colleges or universities—all except Dartmouth, that is.

Rowing was a popular sport at East Lyme High School in Connecticut. Thanks to a local wealthy man, Fred Emerson (who funded the rowing program), 200 of the school's 1,200 students participated on the team. A benefactor of several high school and college teams, Emerson was one of the most important people in the United States regarding the development of women's rowing. He truly cared about involving the local youth in the sport. Luckily for Scott, he was one of the "local youth" who benefitted from Emerson's generosity. Scott immediately connected with the sport his freshman year of high school. "It was the only sport where I noticed a strong correlation between effort and results. I liked everything about it from the start," Scott says. And colleges liked everything about his skill in rowing… except for Dartmouth, the one school he wanted to attend.

After applying for early admission to Dartmouth and getting wait-listed, Scott took matters into his own hands, soliciting a half dozen *additional* letters of recommendation, for a total of nine. Finally, he was admitted. But while he had scholarships to every other school he'd applied to through two different ROTC programs, he received no funding from Dartmouth and wasn't recruited for crew. Knowing his family couldn't afford the tuition, Scott was dejected. He wasn't about to ask his family to make that kind of financial sacrifice.

One day, after receiving all of his letters of acceptance, Scott's dad sat him down. He looked at him seriously and asked, "Scott, where do you *really* want to go?"

Working From Your Values

On the Dartmouth application in 1982, Scott was asked to pick a quote that was meaningful to him. He still has the quote sitting on his desk at work, and it tells a lot about what he values and how people contribute to the world:

"It is not the critic who counts; not the man who points out how the strong man stumbles, or where the doer of deeds could have done them better. The credit belongs to the man who is actually in the arena, whose face is marred by dust and sweat and blood; who strives valiantly; who errs, who comes short again and again, because there is no effort without error and shortcoming; but who does actually strive to do the deeds; who knows great enthusiasms, the great devotions; who spends himself in a worthy cause; who at the best knows in the end the triumph of high achievement, and who at the worst, if he fails, at least fails while daring greatly, so that his place shall never be with those cold and timid souls who neither know victory nor defeat."

— Theodore "Teddy" Roosevelt, from "Citizenship in a Republic," a speech at the Sorbonne, Paris, April 23, 1910

Scott thought hard and finally decided his father wanted the truth. "I want to go to Dartmouth, but we can't afford that," Scott replied.

His father paused, then said, "We'll find a way. I want you to go to Dartmouth." Scott was elated, but he knew what a tremendous sacrifice the tuition costs would be for his family.

Eventually, they worked it out: his parents agreed to pay one-third, his grandparents offered to pay one-third, and Scott paid the other one-third. Scott later learned that his father had chosen not to go to Dartmouth when he was a young man in part because of his own family's financial position, and he'd always wondered what the road not taken would have been like. In essence, Scott was living two dreams at once: his and his father's. Because of this, Scott approached Dartmouth differently from many of this peers. He felt a sense of obligation to spend those four years training in a profession that would give him employable skills and lead to a lucrative profession, in no small part so he could give his children the chance to go to whatever college they might like. He declared a major in engineering and set out to spend four years developing his skills in business, crew, and life.

That fall, Scott tried out for crew and was sent up to train with the junior varsity and varsity crews because of his past rowing experience, while the rest of the freshman athletes spent their time learning the technique of the sport. Freshmen must row on the freshmen team in the spring, according to Ivy League rules, but oarsmen with exceptional high school rowing experience are sometimes sent to row with the varsity crews in the fall. "I realized in those couple of months that I could potentially row on varsity and be competitive," Scott explains. "That was an exciting discovery, except I was also really segmented from the rest of the freshman team. While they were all learning the skill of getting the oar in and out of the water, they were also getting to know each other and forming friendships." When Scott was moved back to the freshman boat just before a race against Yale, he felt separated from them. He decided that, to become accepted within the team, he had to do his best and set an example—and not focus on the fact that he'd been rowing for years. It wasn't long before Scott was elected team captain, a true honor since he hadn't spent much time with the other athletes.

As his coach, I quickly noticed that Scott had tremendous knowledge, experience, and technical expertise but didn't put it out on the table. Immediately, he became the most solid athlete in the boat. He knew how to row and his leadership helped cement the team. People looked to him as the one who had skill in the sport, and he quickly became my "coaching backup," helping keep the team levelheaded and motivated, which was of great value to me.

During one particular race at the end of the season, Scott's leadership skills became even more evident. After losing the first heat of the IRA Championship Regatta, which was a blow to team morale, Scott gathered the group together and said, "Look, we're going to go back out there and do the best we can. We know we're not going to win the regatta, now that we didn't make the finals, but we're going to do our best in our final race for places seventh through twelfth." The crew responded to Scott's charge and had an exceptional race in the petite finals. Imagine a freshman stepping up like that, in a moment of defeat, and building the team up to do their best. It was really astounding.

About a year later, at the age of nineteen, Scott suffered a debilitating back injury that kept him from rowing for many years. As someone who found such freedom and focus in the sport, who really connected to crew on a fundamental level, this crushed him. But he was never one to walk away from his greatest desires, and like his commitment to Dartmouth, he kept up his therapies and hoped to row again. He still wanted to achieve his lifelong dream of rowing in the Henley Royal Regatta, one of the most prestigious rowing events in the world, which takes place on the River Thames each year in Henley, England.

Several years later, in the fall of 1989, Scott was living in London. While having lunch with a client, the topic of crew came up. "Scott, I didn't know you like to row," his client said. "I still row at the London Rowing Club. If you're interested, show up any Sunday at 8:00 a.m., and we'll get you in a boat."

By then, Scott's back was much better, so he decided to give it a try. He arrived at the club, got in the boat, and began rowing—and didn't feel any pain! Right away, he began rowing six days a week with the team. Even though he was working full time as an entrepreneur, he showed up for two practices a day, morning and evening. He was tired but happy. And it didn't hurt that the team was good, either. They'd won several races locally and planned to compete for Scott's dream race: The Henley Royal Regatta.

Selecting Great Leaders

"It takes a long time to help people get to where I am, and it's very hard," Scott explains. "The first thing I do is determine if somebody has the stamina, the raw horsepower, the determination, and the patience to compete at this level. It's at least a ten-year process, and most people don't have the constitution for that. So, I look carefully to select the kinds of people who have the wherewithal and motivation to do it, and then they have to be a good cultural fit; they have to be team players."

One beautiful July afternoon a couple of days before the Henley qualifying heats, Scott was helping carry the boat back to the boathouse after practice. Suddenly, he felt pain shoot through his body like a bolt of lightening had struck him from out of the sky. He collapsed on the ground and couldn't move, his back in excruciating pain, completely immobilized. He spent the next four days in bed, hardly able to move. Meanwhile, Neil, a teammate who hadn't made the boat, substituted for him to get through the Henley qualifying rounds. After they made the qualifying rounds, Neil came to see Scott.

"Scott," Neil said, "If there's ever a point between now and the Henley Regatta where you feel like getting back in the boat—even a single race—that seat is yours." Scott knew how unselfish an offer this was, considering Neil was the person who had qualified. But Neil knew how important the race was to Scott. It was Scott's dream, one he may never have the chance to accomplish again in his life, and Neil knew that. Besides, Neil had rowed at Henley several times before and, as a British native, expected to have that opportunity again.

The day before the race, Scott gave it one last shot and went to an osteopath. "Look, doc, the dream of my life happens tomorrow on the Thames River," Scott said. "If there's anything you can do—I don't care what it is—do it, as long as it doesn't do any permanent damage." The doctor did have an option: acupuncture. He placed tiny needles in Scott's back, hooked them up to electrodes, and an hour later, Scott walked out pain free.

The next day, Neil fulfilled his promise, graciously stepping down and letting Scott take his seat in the boat.

"I rowed in the Henley Royal Regatta," Scott recalls. "We lost because I was too hesitant on the start. We got down a length and never came back. But I got to row at Henley. That was my dream."

Scott never forgot the kindness of his teammate, and Neil's selflessness became an integral part of Scott's approach to business. In 2011, Scott's firm was competing to win the opportunity to invest in Blue Jeans Network, a video communications company. Most of the top firms were vying for the opportunity to invest. Thankfully, Scott's reputation in the industry preceded him, particularly one of his earlier successes with a similar company.

The Blue Jeans Network team felt his experience was very relevant. But for this deal, he was really in a supporting role; his colleague, Jon Sakoda, was trying to win it on his own. At the very end, after everything was negotiated, Blue Jeans Network came back to Jon and said, "Look, Jon, the deal is yours. But you're not the board member—it has to be Scott."

Jon was understandably disappointed—after all, it was his deal—but he knew he had no choice but to give the spot to Scott. The two talked through the details. Scott said, "I'll do it, but I want you to know one thing, Jon: If this company is a failure, I'll take all the blame. But if there's ever a moment at any time in the future, no matter how wildly successful this company is, if there's ever an opportunity to take over the board seat, it's yours, without question." This was Scott's opportunity to give back what Neil had given to him those many years ago at Henley.

Almost two years later, it became clear that Blue Jeans Network would become a very successful company, and due to his increased responsibilities at NEA, Scott asked the CEO, Krish Ramakrishnan, if he would allow Scott to give his board seat to Jon. Without hesitation, Krish said that Jon would be a welcome board member in place of Scott. Scott promised to support the company and to help Jon, and the deal was struck. From Scott's perspective, it was a generous offer on Krish's part, and he was thankful Jon had earned Krish's respect and trust. Scott walked away from the meeting remembering Neil's generosity all those years ago on the lawn at Henley, and how much it had meant to him to have his dream of rowing at Henley come true.

Just like his work with Jon and the Blue Jeans Network, Scott looks for opportunities to let others shine daily. "The amount you can accomplish is inversely proportional to the recognition you require for it," he explains, and this statement holds true in every aspect of his professional life. He has taken the many sacrifices made on his behalf to heart—his parents' willingness to make Dartmouth work, even though it was beyond their means; his teammate's sacrifice to let him recognize his dream of rowing at Henley. In fact, I've had the good fortune of being Scott's business coach, so I've witnessed just how effective—and yet humble—Scott is as a leader.

Recently, I sat in on a meeting Scott was charged with running and saw him in action. Unlike some leaders, Scott took a backseat role in leading this meeting. Instead of commanding attention, he let others take the floor and bring their ideas forward. He listened. He didn't need to be the figurehead or the person with all the answers. Instead, he asked questions and allowed others to speak. As a result, in this particular meeting, there was great debate, ideological conflict, and challenge throughout, and Scott sat there calmly, facilitating the meeting so that the conflict would lead to a decision with greater buy-in from the team.

"In crew, you can't win if everybody isn't pulling together in a very precise way and giving it all their effort," Scott explains. "The margins of victory are very small and won by extraordinary effort on the day of the race, as well as from the training that leads up to it, which is an enormous amount of sacrifice. You can't get that out of people if they haven't really bought in, and that's true in the venture capital business. It's a highly competitive field, and if you operate at a scale like we do, it's a team sport, too, because no matter how great anyone's individual investments might be, they won't be enough to result in world-class performance for our investors. That's why it's paramount to get people to buy in to decisions and to learn and develop themselves in a way that someday they won't need my help, which means making sure they get the chance to lead."

In his everyday business interactions, Scott looks for ways to let others shine while focusing on building others up, rather than putting himself in the center. Jon Sakoda is just one example, but there are many others.

The Importance of Trusting Your Instincts

"Venture capital investing is very risky business. Investment decisions are made with little information and tremendous uncertainty," Scott says. "They are commitments that last almost a decade on average and are usually made in a few weeks or months, sometimes in a single day. Analysis only gets you so far, and at the end of the day, you have to trust your instincts. And the best investments are often the least obvious, because they are brand new inventions that don't compare to anything, have no market by definition (we like to say we invest in huge markets that don't exist yet), and they often involve unproven entrepreneurs who have not yet shown that their invention will work!

"Looking back after 17 years, I sometimes wonder if I have any business doing what I am doing—it is just too hard. I feel like the man on the wire, and I know I shouldn't look down. Inevitably, the spectacular failures humble you again and again, but you have to pick yourself up and get back in the boat, ready to give everything you have to win."

Whit's Words

Scott knew the importance of giving others opportunities to shine. As he put it, "The amount you can accomplish is inversely proportional to the recognition you require for it." He also knew that letting others shine begins with *where* they can shine. As a leader, you need to give those you lead a clear, strategic understanding of where and how their strengths line up with the mission of the organization. Once those strengths are identified, you must help them see where they have the capabilities and motivation to excel.

Be generous with your trust of your team's abilities from the beginning. This act of trust will create a greater degree of engagement, allow freedom of expression, encourage ideas, and empower your team to open up and utilize their full potential. By doing so, you also create an opportunity for yourself to let go of control, and sometimes letting go can have the most influence.

The value of letting others shine gives them the impetus to step up and take on more responsibility, more authority, and more accountability for your agreed-to commitments. It allows creativity of thought and lessens the fear of failure or fear of retribution if things don't go as planned...which they never do. It instills a sense of courage to speak up and challenge leadership, challenge teammates, and challenge the status quo in times of stress and uncertainty. It shows them a leader who exhibits humility. Humility is one of the greatest assets leaders can practice for the purpose of inspiring others to excel.

What can you do to begin this process of letting others shine? How can you inspire upcoming leaders and those with high potential to become fully engaged, motivated, and inspired, while empowering them to take on more authority? Here are some tips for creating an avenue for achievement at the highest level:

1. Make space for people to shine. Be deliberate in doing so, and give them the freedom to show their strengths without giving them too much instruction.

2. Become more strategically observant. Observe what your young leaders are doing by keeping informational cards on them, their interactions, and their commitment with you and others.

3. Make time to be around your people. Practice "do with" leadership. Do more *with* them instead of them doing things *for* you.

4. Set the right culture. This brings out the best in you and your team.

5. Look for opportunities to praise. Be specific with your comments and tell them the impact of their good work on you and others.

Wolf-Dietrich Weber

Igniting Personal Contribution

About Wolf

Wolf-Dietrich Weber joined Google in 2004 and quickly rose to the role of principal engineer, putting him in the top 1 percent of the company's engineers. Specifically, he focuses on issues associated with large-scale datacenter deployments; much of the work he is involved in indirectly affects hundreds of millions of people across the globe. His senior-level role involves brainstorming and implementing new ideas, while also managing a team of talented people. As a leader, he has a group-driven mentality: each person's ideas and insights are valuable, and everyone must take responsibility for the project as a whole. It's his belief in bottom-up creative strategy, in which ideas come from the team rather than being directed from leaders. He also instills a strong sense of responsibility to all who work with him. These attributes help to set Wolf apart in his field.

Prior to Google, Wolf worked in the electrical engineering field with large-scale multiprocessors. His first job out of his PhD program was at HAL Computer Systems, a startup aimed at replacing mainframes with much cheaper microprocessor-based computers. After six years at HAL, he joined Sonics, another startup company in Mountain View, California, where he worked on system-on-chip design. The company has since had a large impact on the system-on-chip market, including a good deal of cell phone and other consumer electronics chips. He was there for five years before joining Google.

He graduated with a BA in engineering and computer science from Dartmouth, a BE from the Thayer School of Engineering, and a PhD in electrical engineering from Stanford University. He and his wife, Veronique, enjoy traveling the world. The two currently live in San Jose, California. In his free time, Wolf enjoys flying gliders and power planes, has a commercial rating in gliders, and owns a half share in a single-seat glider.

Getting to Google

Wolf-Dietrich Weber was born and raised in Germany and went to high school in Singapore but wanted to go to college in the United States. He dreamed of the educational and career opportunities related to computers that awaited him in the United States, opportunities he wouldn't have in his native country. While he worked hard and had the knowledge and skill to get into high-level universities like MIT and Caltech, his family didn't have the financial resources. Since college was essentially free in Germany, Wolf's dad wanted him to go to school there. Not one to be deterred, Wolf decided to apply to top-level US schools, hoping an opportunity would allow him to pursue his dreams. Knowing his desire to head stateside, his math teacher recommended that Wolf apply to Dartmouth. While Dartmouth hadn't been a consideration, he connected with the alumni association in Singapore and started learning about their top-notch engineering school. After submitting his application, he anxiously awaited a decision, hoping he would be able to fund his education.

And then the news came. He was accepted to Dartmouth! His dream was so close, but he still didn't have a way to pay for tuition, even with the financial aid the college was offering. "I had resigned myself that I likely wouldn't be able to go to the United States," Wolf explains. "But then a generous and loyal Dartmouth alum came through town, and the Dartmouth alumni club in Singapore hooked me up with him. They told him, 'Wolf wants to go to Dartmouth but doesn't have enough financial aid. Isn't there something you can do?'" A few days later, Wolf received a telegram from Dartmouth, which read, "We found some more money; won't you come to Dartmouth?" After years of dreaming of studying abroad, Wolf finally made his way to the United States.

During freshman week, as he was walking across campus, taking in the sights and sounds of his new country of residence, he saw the crew shell sitting in slings on the Dartmouth Green. As he walked up to the shell, the team captain motioned to Wolf, eyed his six-foot-seven-inch frame and then asked, "Have you ever seen one of these before?" He pointed to a shell. "How would you like to row?" Although Wolf had never rowed before, he decided to give crew a try. After all, what did he have to lose? He had already moved across the world and left everything he knew behind for an exciting adventure at his dream school. Why not try something new? That week, he joined the Dartmouth rowing team.

Like many of his teammates who hadn't rowed before, Wolf was nervous as he learned the sport of rowing. He soon found it gave him the chance to physically push himself in a way he couldn't in other sports. He enjoyed being a part of a team and working together, moving the boat through the water, oars and bodies rowing in sync, relying on the others in the boat to give their best efforts. He especially liked going on the road for races, and there was a unique joy in the group.

I remember traveling from Hanover to a race at Syracuse, which was six hours one way. At some point along the New York State thruway, Wolf wandered up to my seat with a pensive look on his face. "Coach," he said, "I'm not traveling on this bus for twelve hours to go all the way out to Syracuse and back to lose a six-minute crew race!" He left me sitting there, astonished, and returned to his seat in the back of the bus. We didn't lose the next day, as we handled Syracuse well on their water. I loved that about Wolf—he wasn't going to lose because it would have been a waste of his valuable time.

Probably most important to Wolf, crew was his first experience of being part of a team, and I was his first coach. "I didn't really play any sports in high school, so Whit was my first experience working with a coach," he explains. "And one of the things he instilled in us was this sense of working together as a team. That was really important for me. He always had a positive outlook and made us work hard. But it wasn't as though he was a slave driver—he inspired us to *want* to work hard." Coaching Wolf required more of my analytical thought as to how and why I structured the workouts and race plan. He was always searching for information, wanting to understand the thought process behind my coaching decisions. He never challenged me; he just wanted to know. I also taught the athletes to underpromise, but overdeliver—a principle that stayed with Wolf into his later years at Google.

After months of intense winter training, the biggest challenge of the season was upon the Dartmouth freshman class of '86 team: the Yale race. Yale traditionally had fast crews, and the Dartmouth team knew they weren't going to be easy to beat.

We arrived on the Yale campus late in the day in early March. The athletes had never been to Yale, with its Gothic buildings covered in ivy and the busy streets of downtown New Haven, Connecticut. It was a far cry from the small town of Hanover, New Hampshire. The next morning, the twenty-minute ride to the boathouse was quiet. We had prepared all winter for this race, and much of my focus during the long winter training workouts had been to use the Yale race as the one to win. If we could beat Yale early in the season, it would give us the confidence to race fast the rest of the spring season.

The day was overcast, cold, wet, and dreary. The Yale course is on a swiftly flowing river with a turn 500 meters into the race. As I looked around before the race, I realized that we were surrounded with "Yalies" coming to watch their Bulldogs beat up on the Dartmouth crew. You could tell from the way the Yale athletes carried themselves around the boathouse, they thought it was going to be an easy victory for them.

The strategy was clear: Get a good solid start and move out early to see if we could gain some confidence and rattle them early on. Get to the 1000-meter mark (halfway) and see where we stood against the Bulldogs. Take another strong, hard twenty strokes rowing from ahead. Get ahead and stay ahead! Don't come back to the dock with anything left in the tank. Beat Yale!

When I finally saw the Dartmouth crew come around the turn ahead of Yale, I felt a quiet exhilaration. We had done it! We went on to hold them off. We beat Yale by open water on their course. It was a fantastic feeling, and the entire boathouse went quiet. That freshman boat was the only Dartmouth victor that day. I knew we had a boat that would be competitive all year. But the team didn't know what they had just accomplished.

In crew, there is a long-held tradition of betting shirts, in which the crew that loses the race has the difficult task of walking over to the winning crew and handing them their shirts. The losing coxswain hands his shirt to the winning coxswain, and so on. Most crews now bring new "betting shirts" to hand to the victors rather than using their racing shirts, as they did in the earlier years of racing. But nonetheless, when a team wins, they expect shirts from the losing team.

After the exhilarating win, the Dartmouth freshman team looked over and waited for their prize; I had prepared them for both how to be humble in accepting shirts and how to be gracious in losing their shirts. The team grew excited at their reward—not only had they beaten Yale, but they were getting great shirts out of it, too. They couldn't wait to enjoy the moment where their Yale counterparts would have to bring their betting shirts over, shake hands, and congratulate the Dartmouth winners. This tradition is long-standing and unspoken between crews. It always happens very shortly after a race.

But as the teams cleaned up after the race, it became clear that there were no shirts coming their way. In fact, the Dartmouth team learned that the Yale team hadn't even brought betting shirts with them to the course that day. Maybe they hadn't expected to lose, but it was a really poor show of sportsmanship on Yale's part. I was informed that they'd mail us their betting shirts. This was unheard of and disappointing, as I had promised my oarsmen that this was the prize they would receive. Not only did we not receive the shirts, but none of the Yale oarsman even came over to shake hands or congratulate us for the victory. This had never happened before in my coaching career, and the Dartmouth athletes were disappointed and disillusioned. I hoped their trust in me had not been affected, as this had been the carrot all winter long: to win a Yale betting shirt!

Getting the shirts in the mail weeks later brought me feelings of both anger and excitement. It was like receiving a gold medal after the games are over. I wasn't sure how to give out the prized shirts, as I wanted to make sure they understood the significance of the event. "When the shirts finally came in the mail, Whit took us behind the boathouse and gave them to us, rather than in front of the other Dartmouth oarsmen, since we were the only ones getting shirts," Wolf recalls. "It was understated, and that's very much in line with what I value about myself."

The team grew excited as I reached into the box to pull out the first jersey: a low-quality, dark-blue shirt with a little white "Y" printed on it. I handed each shirt out with the ceremonial handshake and "good row" comment, which had been forgotten by the Yalies. "As far as betting shirts were concerned, they were pretty much the low end of what you could get," Wolf explains. "But we were very excited to get them." To this day, I think those nine guys learned more about sportsmanship from how the whole event unfolded than they did from winning the race. I was very proud of how we all handled ourselves.

Years later, in 2004, after Wolf graduated from Dartmouth, finished his PhD at Stanford, and worked at two startup companies, colleagues from Stanford suggested that he come work at a growing company called Google. While the company sounded intriguing, he felt it was outside of his expertise. After all, he thought, Google was mostly a software company—a field far removed from the world of computer system and system-on-chip design. After encouragement from his colleagues, he decided to give the company a try.

Surprisingly, he fit right in at Google. Stepping into a new area of engineering proved to be an enjoyable challenge, and he soon learned that all of the great things he'd heard about Google were true: The company has an exceptional work environment where every person is valued. Many ideas bubble up from the bottom, rather than being conceptualized and implemented from the top. All Google locations—including "Googleplex" in Mountain View, California—reflect the company's inspiration-centered approach and unique culture. The company strives to create an environment of creativity, from Google Maps-inspired wall murals in Hyderabad, India, to an outdoor-themed collaborative space, complete with a rowboat, lawn chairs, and trees, in London, United Kingdom. Google locations even have cafes serving made-from-scratch and organic dishes like red beet ravioli with tarragon, cashew filling, and yellow pepper purée. Aside from the unique interior design, delicious food, and collaborative culture, employees work on exciting and interesting projects—concepts that touch literally billions of people. They influence Google users each and every day, enhancing their lives and offering new, innovative ways to approach work and play.

Benefit Each Team Member

"People usually make choices about whom they want to be as leaders by going after their own self-interest," Wolf says. "They ask questions. Can this person do something for me? Is this the way that this group and I are going to be successful?

"It usually does not work to enforce from the top-down, because people will just end up leaving if they can. There are some rare circumstances where people are forced to stay or accept the conditions as they are, but most of the time, when people are unhappy about the leadership of the group, they'll go somewhere else, or they'll figure out another way of doing things.

"If you're looking to be an effective leader, you have to make sure you're doing something that is beneficial to each individual on your team, and that the people you're trying to lead will actually derive benefits from your leadership, see that their points of view are taken into account, and know that they'll have a way of influencing decisions."

Wolf's role as principal engineer has given him the opportunity to lead in a way that positively influences both his team and himself. He truly cares about those he leads, and Google's values are right in line with Wolf's own beliefs about leadership. "I think one thing people often have a misconception about is, if you become a senior manager and have a team to lead, you get more power and your team has to serve you. The reality is actually the other way around, especially in a company like Google," Wolf says. "In general, your job is to make sure that the people you're leading are actually happy, because if they're not, they're going to take off, and you won't be leading them anymore. You have to make sure you actually serve the people you wish to lead." Wolf exemplifies being honest, up front, and open about everything he does in his leadership role. Most of all, he believes leadership should be driven by what his team wants and needs. People must *want* to follow and trust the person leading; this is achieved by putting others first. This includes accepting people's imperfections, including his own.

His leadership style is about more than just reciprocity or the Golden Rule—Wolf believes everyone needs to go out of his or her way to help with the common good…and the team's good. Taking responsibility for projects as a whole is one way to do this. For example: Assume a person is working on a project, and she notices a small rubber piece wasn't made. It's not part of her job to make the piece, but she knows if it isn't completed, the entire project will fail. In cases like this, Wolf says that person should take personal responsibility and finish it for the good of the team and company. People must step outside themselves to complete tasks, even if they're not directly assigned to them. This can be applied to many areas of life and has direct implications for his team at Google.

In many ways, Wolf's leadership has also been influenced by the work ethic he developed at Dartmouth. Rowing on the Dartmouth crew was his first time both being coached and belonging to a team. It was there he learned the importance of teamwork, developed a profound work ethic that combined hard work and recovery, and formed a positive outlook even when things did not go as planned, like in the Yale race. As a teammate on such a talented team, Wolf had to be humble and put in the work in training, yet on race day, courageously rise to the occasion of taking on the challenge of beating teams whom had previously been considered unbeatable.

"Being a part of a team at Dartmouth taught me that you can be great, but you certainly can't do things by yourself if you are going to be successful," he says. As he moved through two other professional experiences before joining Google, he learned that you can only be as successful as the people you choose to empower around you. Through his own willingness to step up and help when needed, he inspires those around him and ignites personal contribution—a willingness to work for the good of the team.

Three Questions Every Professional Should Ask to Determine Priorities

When Wolf works with members of his team to help them grow in their careers, he focuses on three overlapping circles, and he says everyone should ask themselves these questions:

1. What do I enjoy doing?

2. What are the areas where I excel?

3. What is valuable to others and how can I make a living providing the value?

An ideal job is the combination of these three things—the area in the center of the three circles. A person must be enjoying himself and doing something he's good at, while providing a service that is valuable to others. "If you can combine those three things together, you're going to be in good shape," Wolf explains.

Whit's Words

Wolf's experience being part of that freshmen eight in 1982 has proved to be an invaluable aspect of his success in developing high-performing teams at Google and previous places of employment. He quickly realized that in order to have a team that is engaged, committed, and performing at a high level, the leader has to be willing to serve the team's needs, not the other way around. As Wolf put it, "You have to make sure you actually serve the people you wish to lead."

When I work with leaders, I ask them to show me their organizational chart with the CEO on the top of the pyramid and the rest of the employees fanning out below at different levels. I ask questions about reporting structures, people's responsibilities, and team functions, among other points. I then take that chart and turn it upside down, so the top leaders are at the bottom, below all those that report to them who are now on top. "This is the way the chart should look! You're working for them! Because if you don't look at it that way, you won't have your position for very long," I state. I encourage you to look at your company's organizational chart the same way. In order for you and your organization to be successful, you need to dedicate your valuable time to meeting the needs of all of those people "above" you on the inverted chart. This quick visual can create an immediate reaction and mind-set shift.

As the leader, are you really clear about the needs and wants of those people who have the most impact and leverage into making you or the company successful? What can you do to increase their levels of engagement, ownership, responsibility, and accountability for results?

Google encourages ideas from any and all within the company. Dartmouth Printing, a local company in Hanover, New Hampshire, has been using this technique for years. When employees come up with ideas that help save or make money for the company, the employees are compensated with a percentage of the savings or profits. One way to inspire ideas is to create incentives and have leaders encourage thoughts and ideas anytime, anywhere, on anything. Once you start to include people and offer incentives for their thoughts, ideas, and opinions, they're much more invested in the company and in working for you as a leader, and their motivation goes up because they're constantly looking for ways to improve the systems in your organization. When people feel valued, it increases the value of the organization.

John Adair, one of the world's thought leaders on leadership, shares a very simple model that includes three overlapping circles. I have included it below.

Team Leadership Model

ACCOMPLISHING
TASKS

BUILDING
TEAM

MEETING
INDIVIDUAL NEEDS

Task: Completing the task
Team: Building and maintaining a team
Individual: Meeting the needs of the individuals on the team

I have used the three circle model for years in my
with leaders. When I see leaders spending too much
in the task circle, I ask them how well the task is being
Usually, if leaders are too involved in the task circle, t
aware of the other two circles, team and individual. How c
build a highly effective team if the leader is buried in the ta
By being too task-focused, they are not giving others a ch
develop. They are neglecting the individual needs of others, c
lack of trust and low work engagement.

As Wolf has discovered, in order to build teams, you not
need to set a clear direction and get agreement on the goals–
certain situations, you need to be aware of the individual needs
each of the team members, and other times you need to step up an
create a team. As a leader, if the task at hand isn't being accomplished
avoid diving in your helicopter into the task circle. Pull up and get a
better view from 10,000 feet and see if your task would be better
served by serving your people. Are their needs being met and are
you creating situations to build and maintain team behavior and
performance? How can you take the diversity of talents you have in
your organization, similar to what we had on the '86 Crew, and create
a team that will outperform the competition that has been beating
you for years? How can you get the shirts off their backs?

Mike Rich

*Determined to Discover
Your Own Values*

About Mike

Mike Rich is an associate professor of Japanese language, literature, and culture and the program coordinator of Japanese and Asian Studies at Georgetown College in Kentucky. With a penchant for international living, he spent short periods living in Nepal and Mexico and lived in Asia for a total of seven years, including six years in Japan. His interest in the Japanese martial arts of kendō (Japanese fencing), kyūdō (Japanese archery), and a theatrical form called nogakū brought him and his family back to Japan for a yearlong sabbatical in 2012.

After graduating from Dartmouth with a BA in Asian Studies, Mike completed his MA in Asian Studies at Yale University and returned to Yale to complete his PhD in East Asian languages and literature. At Dartmouth, he spent his junior year abroad as an exchange student at Keio University where he practiced with the Keio crew. After his year in Japan, he traveled in Western China and Tibet, and revisited the village in Nepal where he had worked in high school.

When he's not immersing himself in Asian culture, Mike enjoys hunting and fishing with his two daughters, Laura and Angelica, and spending time with his wife, Fumi. He currently lives with his family in Georgetown, Kentucky, on a thirty-four-acre farm.

International Discovery

Palo Alto is known for being one of the most expensive cities in the United States and home to big technology companies like Hewlett-Packard. It's a place many dream of living. But to young Mike Rich, moving from Colorado to California at the age of five was like moving to a new country, a place he felt he'd never belong. The family first moved to Sunnyvale, more of a working class neighborhood at that time with lots of orchards. Now, Silicon Valley dominates the area. When Mike was in the eighth grade, the family moved to Palo Alto. Mike says, "The first month we moved into our house in Palo Alto, we biked to school from our grandparents' home in Menlo Park, through the wealthiest sections of Palo Alto, making a vivid impression." The demand from his family and the high-pressure environment was too much, and he knew he'd never be able to fit into the ideals of those around him. He felt overwhelming pressure from his family and community to be a "success"—a doctor, lawyer, tech genius, or another equally impressive title. Luckily, Mike has never been one to accept others' values as his own.

In high school, while many of his peers were spending time at the local hangout and dreaming of their future careers, Mike spent a life-changing four months in the Himalayan foothills in Nepal. As he lived and worked alongside the natives—mostly poor, barefoot villagers—he came to love the beauty of the people, their toughness and resilience, and especially their generosity. He marveled at the stark contrast between the village and Palo Alto. Each day, he went to different farmhouses, and the Nepalese served whatever food they had, even though they had very little; the entire time he was there, he ate mostly rice and lentils and mustard greens. Mike remembers, "I had water buffalo once while working on a different project in a different village but never in the village where I lived (Nagarkot). Water buffalo were far too precious to be eaten." As a rare luxury, the farmers boiled milk and made what tasted like a sweet cream cheese. The houses were made out of stone and mud, and often there was a cavity in the house containing a beehive. "They would reach in and pull out a comb of honey for me as a little treat," Mike recalls.

As he lived among those tough and kind people, they quickly became his role models. Working with them on their farms, he started to notice that while they weren't doctors, lawyers, or technology experts like the people back home, they were following their own set of values—values far removed from the success-driven world. "It made me realize that Palo Alto was not the center of the world, and I was not the center of the world," Mike says. "There were many other worlds out there." He felt at peace in this place so far removed from what he knew in California.

Returning home after his experience in Nepal was difficult for Mike. He wanted to reject everything around him, but he didn't know how. He felt different from his high school classmates and became angry and rebellious. The pressures from his family only pushed him further away, and he wanted nothing more than to be free from it all.

Although he was planning on eventually attending UCLA, Mike decided to take a "gap year" off from school to travel. First, he moved to the San Joaquin Valley where he worked alongside Mexican laborers in 114 degree weather, trimming avocado trees and sorting hundreds of turkeys a day. "I gained an appreciation for using the physical to heal the mental," Mike says. "It was grueling work, but it provided a good feeling of well-being and grounding, too." He also realized that he'd been too caught up in success and prestige, and yet here were these good people, making $4.00 an hour, living in less-than-ideal situations—but they seemed happier, in a way, than the "successes" he knew back home.

A few months after returning to Palo Alto from San Joaquin Valley, and still on his gap year, Mike and 12 friends decided to ride their bicycles across the country. Young and excited, they drove to Washington, D.C., in a van, and then had a small ceremony before setting out to ride across the country. Since it was already November when they began the ride, the group kept south during their journey. Not only was the experience physically challenging, but it also helped him see that not everyone lived a high-pressure life. Just like in Nepal and San Joaquin Valley, Mike was introduced to a whole new culture—Southern culture—and he was fascinated by how different it was from Palo Alto. "In South Carolina, there were guys just sitting out in front of their houses, and it looked like they had been sitting out front for years," Mike says, laughing. "They usually would get up to come talk to us and ask us what we were doing and where we were going."

Implementing the Japanese Way

Mike's values closely align with those of the Japanese. "One thing that really strikes me about Japanese culture is that it's much more group oriented," he says. "So leaders tend not to be superstar types. They tend to really expend much of their energy developing a team or personal bonds between people. They do a lot of taking care of people, nurturing, and making many personal sacrifices to help others. It's something I really admire."

Shortly after returning from his cross-country bicycle ride, he went to Mexico to help build schools and became very close with his host family. Mike loved the beautiful, mountainous village; it was a simple, serene place. Kids in the village herded sheep and Mike would sometimes go up into the mountains with them. It reminded him of Nepal: village children all playing together, a rural calmness about the place. There was something that affected Mike deeply about the town, a peacefulness he would try to recreate in his own life for many years to come.

After returning to Palo Alto, Mike was set to go to UCLA, which he'd chosen mostly because his parents could afford to send him there. But then he got some unexpected news: his grandmother offered to pay for college. He could choose anywhere in the country, so he went to his high school counselor and the two pulled out a college catalog. He ended up applying to Williams and Dartmouth. Mike explains, "I never did the Williams interview. It turned out later that my great-uncle had gone to Dartmouth, and everybody on my maternal grandmother's side of the family had gone there. So, I actually had a connection to it, although I didn't know that at the time." He went to the entrance interview, got accepted, and made his way east. And being unconcerned with status, he didn't even realize he was attending an Ivy League school until the bus ride up to Hanover, when another classmate mentioned the college's elite status.

The year of travel, new experiences, and building self-awareness helped Mike see there was more to life than living for success, money, and prestige. He wanted a life that meant more than that, a life lived according to *his* values. While he wasn't yet sure what his values were, Nepal had sparked an interest in Asian culture, and it was something he wanted to explore further. He also yearned for camaraderie and connection, something that had been hard for him to achieve since he was so different from many of his peers in Palo Alto. What better way to push and achieve these goals than by joining crew, a sport that was not only demanding but also required the team to become one unit, to work in sync?

Influenced by author Yukio Mishima, specifically his writings about group physical activity, Mike decided to give crew a try. Since he'd spent so much time alone, especially bicycling, he looked forward to being part of a group again. He'd played water polo competitively in high school, and he was looking for something that would let him connect with a group of his peers in a similar way. "It was very exciting to be with a group of other guys in the same boat," he says. "That was a neat feeling."

When Mike came to the first crew practice that freshman year at Dartmouth, he had a calmness and lightness about him. Mike was a curious soul, and his interest in the Far East helped me understand his quiet, introspective nature. His easygoing personality and sense of humor made it easy for me to work with him. I knew he wasn't aware of the potential he possessed for both his physical and emotional fortitude. He was built to be a rower, but he hadn't been pushed to his limits. I couldn't wait to help him find this unreached power. At times, I had to figure out how to help him see his greatness. What limited him early on was his inability to know how far and how hard to push himself.

At first, being in the boat felt very limiting and confining to Mike. He was strapped in, his movement restricted, like he was a link in a chain; it was certainly a contrast to the movement of trimming avocado trees or bicycling across the country, the freedom of moving his body however he wanted. Each stroke he made affected the rest of the team and the movement of the boat, and that took time to get used to. But he learned to enjoy the synchronicity of crew, and especially the experience of rowing. "It was such a scenic river," Mike recalls. "We would paddle upstream, and there were green fields and cows and farmhouses. The autumn leaves were falling in the river." He was inspired to write poetry about the beauty of being on the water, the mist hovering directly over the water in the early spring, and the fluid movement of the boat along the river.

Of course, most worthwhile experiences have a struggle attached, and, for Mike, that struggle was winter training. "It was very cold and just going outside was a gritty experience. And yet, there we were, working out," he explains. "I guess it was the persistence in the midst of bleakness that was somehow memorable." For a while, it was a struggle for Mike to even run a mile relay, even though he'd done track in high school. But then he started to notice how fit he was becoming and that he was able to push himself to an athletic place he'd never been. "At least for me, personally, it gave me a lot of confidence," he says. He knew if he could get through winter training, he could get through anything.

That winter, I wrote a one-page handwritten evaluation for each of the crew members. My evaluation of Mike said, among other things, that he was "very quiet but explosive." For Mike, it was one of the first evaluations of that kind he'd received, and the page I'd written detailing his quiet strength stuck with him later in life. "That piece of paper Whit provided each of us was really important, and it was very new to me," Mike says. "Whit's coaching style was very strict, and he had very high expectations he presented in a very soft way."

After college, Mike did what I always knew he'd do: pave his own path. After completing his master's degree in Asian studies at Yale, he went to Taiwan to learn Chinese. Later, to conduct research for his PhD dissertation, he moved to Tokyo where he finally discovered what he had hoped for all along, a way of life that worked best for him. "The Japanese culture has supported me in some ways because the dominant culture in Japan fits my way of being more," Mike explains. "I always felt like I should be the corporate CEO superstar type. I never have been able to be that way. In Japan, I don't have to be that way. I'm valued for who I am."

After returning from Japan to finish his PhD at Yale and teaching for a number of years, Mike began to wonder if he had chosen the right career path. While he was happy studying about Asian culture, he wasn't sure if he should teach and questioned if pursuing a PhD had been the right choice for him—or if he'd just wasted his time. So, he hired a career coach, a man who would prove instrumental in helping Mike.

The coach asked a series of questions and talked through some of the struggles Mike was having. One question got right to the heart of what he had been wondering: are you happy with who you are, or would you rather be someone else? After considering the question, Mike decided he was very happy with who he was, and this helped him accept the path he'd chosen. "I realized it's not some huge identity question or identity search," he says. "These are the skills you have, this is a job you can get, go ahead and get it and do it, and all the while keep your eyes open and mind open about other things you could do." Life is long and options are endless, and there are no limits to what a person can do. Mike realized he could always make other decisions later, and he has remained open to any new opportunities and experiences. In essence, he learned to find peace in the everyday—to love and accept life as it comes.

But Mike's coach had an even greater impact. "My career coach also talked about how 'life is sweetest when you're living according to your values,'" he explains. "I'd been struggling, but I'd never really articulated the core of the struggle. It was about affirming my own values. I'd never thought of it in that way." This idea has since become a part of Mike's everyday life, something that helps him make choices according to the values he has, the things that matter to him. And quality of life is first and foremost for Mike.

Today, Mike and his family live on a thirty-four-acre farm. It's a hilly property with woods, meadows, and ponds—a beautiful setting for his daughters to enjoy their childhood. He has also been able to narrow down what he values most, the things that define who he is and who he wants to be: tolerance, acceptance, patience, kindness, generosity, and perseverance. Not surprisingly, these are all words I would use to describe Mike, the man with the quiet strength who isn't afraid to live according to his values.

A New Take on Success

"When I was applying for college at Dartmouth, I had to answer a question about my definition of success. I wrote about the life of Miyamoto Musashi, a famous swordsman," Mike explains. *"I viewed him as successful because he followed his dream of being the best swordsman—he traveled all over Japan, never accepted permanent employment, and was just constantly practicing.*

"Personal success is also being a good person, someone who doesn't harm other people, and being loving and kind. Professional success is having the ability to help others, to make a positive impact on their lives. As Aristotle said, 'Where talents and the needs of the world cross, therein lies your vocation.' So, being able to help somebody—to provide something for someone—would be my view of professional success."

Whit's Words

Values motivate us toward a desired state. Values are principles or standards that create inner satisfaction. Values drive behaviors, and when they're satisfied at work, we have satisfying experiences all day. The opposite happens when values are violated, and poor work behaviors show up as a result. Mike found that when he lives according to his values, he is happier and experiences joy and peace.

Do you know what your values are? Here is a quick way to determine your top values in the context of work.

Step 1:
Think of a very rewarding experience you had at work in the past month.

1. What was the essence of that experience, in a few words?

2. What else was important? Ask this question four to five times until you have four to five values that were present during that experience.

3. If all of those values—the important aspects of that experience—were present each day at work, what would be the total effect at the end of each day?

Step 2:
Think of a recent experience at work that was very dissatisfying, one where you may have felt anger or pain.

1. What was missing, in a few words?

2. What else was missing? Ask this question four to five times until you have four to five values that were missing during that experience.

110

3. Imagine all of those values—the things that were missing—
now being satisfied at work. What would the effect be for
you on a daily basis?

Step 3:

Take all the values you just identified in both exercises and
put them into a cause–effect relationship, top to bottom,
to create your values hierarchy. For example, your value
hierarchy might read: respect, loyalty, trust, honesty,
connection, and integrity. Once you have your hierarchy,
ask these questions:

1. What would my professional life be like if all of my values
were being satisfied on a daily basis at work?

2. What feeling or inner state would my values produce if
they were a regular part of my life? For example, you
might find yourself coming up with words like happiness,
joy, inner peace, and contentment. These feelings are
what you're looking to achieve each day.

Step 4:

To incorporate more of your values into your daily life, write
your values down (in hierarchy order) on a notecard and
post them in a place you will see every day. Then, use them
to guide you in your day-to-day professional life.

1. If you have a very difficult decision to make, look at your
values card and determine which decision would satisfy
more of your values.

2. If you have just had a very dissatisfying day, meeting,
or experience, look at your card and see which values were
violated and which were present.

3. If you want to improve a working relationship with a colleague, team, or customer, use your values to identify which value(s) you need to work with to make the relationship ideal.

Mike found that following his values and passions created positive "inner states" and helped him find peace and happiness. What would your life be like if you lived according to your values? You might be surprised at the transformation it brings at work and at home.

Sam Kinney

Culture Keeping through Self-Awareness and Relationships

About Sam

Sam Kinney is a multitime entrepreneur best known for his work with FreeMarkets in the late '90s. As cofounder and executive vice president of the company, he helped FreeMarkets pioneer online reverse auctions. During a time when many people had never accessed the web, Sam was able to colaunch and build FreeMarkets into a multimillion dollar revenue company. He and primary founder Glen Meakem were winners of the Ernst and Young Entrepreneur of the Year regional award, a high distinction for anyone in business. At age thirty-six, just six years after the company's launch, and ten years after graduating from business school, selling most of his stake in FreeMarkets allowed him to retire.

While Sam has the résumé to work as a top executive, he prefers investing in, and working with, startups. He isn't all business—he's also a devoted father who loves spending time with his large family. Sam graduated from Dartmouth with a BA in economics, cum laude, and was number one in his class at Tuck Business School at Dartmouth, earning his MBA with the highest distinction.

Sam currently lives in Florida with his wife, Wini (also Dartmouth class of '86) and their combined six sons. In his free time, he enjoys fly-fishing, woodworking, home-improvement, and cooking.

Keeper of the Culture

For most kids, spring break means just that—a break. For Sam Kinney, it meant two weeks making maple syrup in northern Ohio. And that didn't count the other four to eight weeks of the sap season when work was squeezed in around school. Harvesting and boiling the sticky, sweet syrup was grueling labor, especially for a teenager, but Sam stuck with it from ages fourteen to eighteen. Each spring, he would prepare himself for the difficult work: taking two white, plastic buckets into the woods, filling them with forty pounds of sap, carrying them 200 yards back through the woods while stepping over snow-covered logs to dump the sap into a large tank. When finished, he'd take his empty buckets back into the woods to repeat the process over again…for hours. Most days would start at 10:00 a.m., once it was warm enough for the sap to flow, and end at 2:00 a.m., when the sap the group had harvested had completed the boiling process. With over 1,000 taps to collect and just a small group of people collecting, this was no easy task. But Sam has always enjoyed a challenge.

Take rowing, for example: Like many of his peers, Sam had never rowed a day in his life when he decided to join the Dartmouth rowing team. In fact, he'd only played a little junior varsity soccer, and neither of his parents were involved in athletics. While the task of becoming an athlete—and trying something challenging and new—would seem a big feat to most, Sam viewed it as an opportunity. What he wasn't expecting was what he would later describe as an "awakening."

His work harvesting sap transitioned perfectly into his work with crew. As he began developing an athlete's body and training for rowing, he was able to bring his work ethic from childhood into adulthood. When he felt so tired he could hardly move another muscle in practice, he remembered the long, fatigued hours harvesting sap during his childhood. When his hands were so shredded from crew practice he could barely hold a pencil in calculus class, he thought about the struggle of hauling two forty-pound buckets of sap and used that memory to push through the residual pain from practice. During practice, he was able to work through those aches and pains as he learned the sport of crew. It was as though his work ethic was maturing, undergoing a metamorphosis. He was no longer a kid in the forest—he was a young man on the water, working hard to achieve a goal.

Sam soon learned that one of the most difficult aspects of any sport—and especially a physically challenging sport like crew—is the practice to game time ratio. It has been said that rowers train 360 hours for thirty-six minutes of competition; although this might be a bit of an exaggeration, it puts into perspective just how much training the class of '86 underwent. "It's all part of a big objective, but that big objective is so far away," Sam explains. "You're training all fall and winter, and you've only got a handful of very short races in the spring." For Sam, the key was learning to enjoy practice. He quickly found that if he didn't focus on enjoying the moment, enjoying training, he would only be content in the sport for a very small amount of time.

With such a positive outlook, it's no wonder Sam was able to make training fun for himself and the rest of the athletes. He would come to practice with a smile on his face and a sense of humor that helped us all get through those long winter months working out in the rowing tanks and weight room and during long runs along wintery roads. He had a way of touching each person with a quip, comment, question, or story. If he saw a teammate struggling to get through an ergometer piece, he would be the one to gather the other athletes around the erg to cheer on their teammate.

Sam was an entrepreneur in the making—he was never bashful and would frequently push back on my demands as a coach. Looking back, I think it was his way of getting the others to rally around a common goal of beating Yale. And while he wasn't the most talented athlete in the first boat, he proved he could push through the pain and hard work. He wanted that seat in the first boat, and he earned it. He was a key component in that boat, bringing hard work, humor, encouragement, and a winning attitude.

As he taught himself to focus on practice and pushed his body physically, Sam started developing a very keen sense of self-awareness.

"Whit helped build some of that self-awareness," he reflects. "His coaching had many points of positive reinforcement with only the occasional corrective point." Early on in his college career, Sam learned to take feedback gracefully, make the needed corrections, and move on. He was not afraid to hear that he needed to do better—rather, he welcomed the feedback because it was the only way he could improve in the sport.

At the end of the fall rowing season, I put together an evaluation of each oarsman's strengths and areas to improve upon for the winter training months. Most of these athletes had never received any kind of written or verbal feedback in their prior high school sports programs, so I was unsure how well they would receive my comments. Sam was open, curious, and willing to make whatever adjustments necessary to get a seat in that first boat. He frequently asked me for extra tips and ideas on how to improve his strength, conditioning, and technique. His openness to my coaching comments put me on my toes, and I found myself paying closer attention during practice so I could give him valuable feedback.

Sam made the first boat for a reason. He pulled hard and constantly encouraged his teammates. Like a goose, he was always honking out support from his seat in the boat. Perhaps the most impressive quality of young Sam, aside from his work ethic, was his ability to build camaraderie. He had a way of keeping the team's spirits high when things were down, whether through a much-needed joke or a light-hearted approach. He sensed what the team needed, responding appropriately to quickly dispel tension and bring the group together as a team. He was able to work with a varied group of people, to relate to them and encourage them—all skills he would later use in entrepreneurial pursuits. In essence, he was the "keeper of the culture," the tie that bound the team together, the one who invested energy into building the team's bond. Many years later, that young man who cared so much about building relationships on the team would be the same one who conceptualized and organized our team reunion in 2011. If it weren't for Sam, the amazing stories of these accomplished men might never have been told.

Relationship building, an appreciation for practice, and self-awareness have served Sam well throughout his life. While these qualities didn't originate with crew, they matured there, and they were transformed into assets that he would later bring into the business world. In 1995, after Sam had been working five years as a management consultant, former General Electric executive Glen Meakem sought him out to cofound and become vice president of FreeMarkets, a company that pioneered the reverse auction, which utilized the Internet to negotiate large industrial and government purchases. During a time when many people didn't have Internet access or even used the web, Sam was faced with a lot of opposition as he worked to get the company up and running. But Sam was never one to back down from a challenge, whether it was harvesting sap, training for crew, or starting a business. That year, the company launched with six employees; five years later, in 2000, they had close to 1,100 employees and twenty-seven offices. Just ten years out of business school, Sam's proceeds from stock sales meant he'd never have to work for anybody else another day in his life.

How does one man accomplish so much in such a short period of time? Sam will be the first to tell you he didn't do it on his own. The relationships he built, both prior to starting FreeMarkets and as they grew the company, were key to his ability to accomplish great things during his time there. When the company was in its infancy, Sam relied on his extensive network of personal and business relationships. "You have to constantly invest in your network," Sam explains. "What it comes down to in huge part is if you are generous with your time for others, all of the sudden you'll find that when you need something, you've got a lot of favors. You've got a lot of people you can reach out and tap, and that's important." Of course, Sam doesn't keep relationships up just for the favors—but he does recognize the importance of reciprocity. So when he and his partner set out to raise money from their existing network, calling everyone they knew to tell them about their incredible venture, it took them just six days to raise $500,000. When the company's revenues hit $91 million in 2000, those investors felt Sam was the one doing *them* the favor.

During the six years he worked at FreeMarkets, Sam became known as the keeper of the culture. Of course, that wasn't a first for Sam—he'd been known as a culture keeper during Dartmouth crew, too. For Sam, culture keeping first starts with an understanding of the company. "You have to first define culture, what it is as an organization you all collectively value in your work," Sam states. "Some of it is work related in terms of technical precision, innovation, and client service. Some of it is values driven in the way you want to behave toward one another. And some of it is values driven or vision driven in terms of what you want the organization to be when it grows up. Some of it is going out and drinking beer with the staff." Not only was he constantly working with individuals on his team to help them understand the vision and how their roles tied into the greater goal of the company, but he also led by example. In fact, Sam worked in nearly every position in the company over those years, from providing product guidance to the technical team, pushing innovations that resulted in a couple dozen patents, writing first marketing materials, to serving as acting CFO for the company's IPO. In each role, he kept the vision of the company at the forefront of his thoughts, while working to build a strong team dynamic—very much like his time in crew.

Sam was steady in his tenacity, drive, and vision keeping—all qualities that aren't easily maintained over an intense six-year period. "When you're an entrepreneur and you're building a business, there's a lot of slogging it out," Sam says. "You don't have the product yet, so you can't go sell it. You have to build it. You have to persevere during those lengthy periods of time when you're not getting any real market feedback. You have to generate your own motivation and use your own intuition."

Practical Insights for Young Entrepreneurs

"If you want to prepare for building a top-level business, keep your lifestyle restrained. Don't go out and buy a five-bedroom house right out of your MBA program. If you want to be an entrepreneur, you're going to be back with ramen noodles for a period of time, so why not just stay on ramen noodles?

"Also, be sure to constantly invest in your network and set a track record people can rely on. When the time came to make those phone calls to fund FreeMarkets, we were able to raise $500,000 in six days because we were calling people who just knew they were going to get that call some-day. It wasn't because we told them, it was because they knew we were going to start a business, we were passionate, and we had set a track record."

Like most entrepreneurs, he had his share of "slogging it out." He once described his work at FreeMarkets as "pushing a rock up a hill." Glen and Sam made presentations at seventy meetings in seventeen cities in nine days for the IPO roadshow. At the end of it, he was exhausted, and some of his colleagues were too tired to even get out of bed. But he pushed through that challenge and got to enjoy an incredible moment: opening NASDAQ when FreeMarkets went public. To this day, that remains a highlight in his life.

The key to maintaining the ability to continue on during the most wearing times, Sam believes, is learning to love practice. Like crew, where the practice to race time is almost laughably unbalanced, a person has to learn to enjoy the preparation, the time spent building the empire. "When you talk about the ratio of practice time to game time in business, the idea is that you have to enjoy all aspects of your job and of being an entrepreneur," Sam explains. "One day you're helping the software team with specs, the next day you're designing a stock option plan, the next day you're writing checks, and the next day you're pitching investors. It's all part of a big objective, and that's the case with rowing, too."

At FreeMarkets, Sam was also known for his ability to build a successful team dynamic. This was in part due to Sam's willingness to self-evaluate and his expectation that his team should do the same. Twice a year, the company would take two days to evaluate the whole company from end to end, including thorough employee evaluations. "One of the things my partner, Glen Meakem, and I would agree on is that the leading cause of death of an executive career is a lack of self-awareness," Sam asserts. In everything he does, Sam strives to be aware of both his strengths and weaknesses.

Once, prior to starting FreeMarkets, Sam was working on a best practices project, setting up a benchmarking day in General Electric's engineering division. He started talking with an engineering manager, who said, "Every time I get a performance appraisal from my boss, I tape it to my office door so everybody can see it." Sam was struck by this, because it showed two things: (1) The manager wasn't afraid to admit that he received negative feedback, and (2) He was not only unafraid of admitting his weaknesses, but he wanted others to know what he was working on so they could help him. This type of attitude is one that Sam strives to bring to work and life, one that he teaches both his employees and his children.

Learning Culture from L.L. Bean

Going into the L.L. Bean flagship store in Freeport, Maine, you can feel the culture as you walk into the store: the way the merchandise is displayed, how you are treated by employees, the return policy. I lost one of my L.L. Bean boots during a canoeing trip down the Allagash River in 1968 when I was twelve years old. When I returned home to Maine, we went back to L.L. Bean to buy a new pair of boots. When I told the salesperson my story, he told me they would make me one boot to replace the one I lost. "No need to buy two boots if you just need one," he said.

Linwood Bean was the person responsible for creating that culture many years ago. If you're at the top of your organization, you have been given the permission, authority, and right to create your organizational culture. Once you can see what others have seen in your leadership behaviors—and change for the better—you will have a greater ability to influence the kind of culture that will bring both you and those you lead satisfaction and success.

When Sam stepped away from the company in 2000, he did so with pride. He knew he'd given his all to FreeMarkets, helping to build a wildly successful company and positively touching many lives in the process. "We had a great, great run at that company. Now, we have an incredible alumni base, and former employees still tell me they've never worked at any place like FreeMarkets." Sam left knowing he'd done everything he could to bring great value to all who worked at FreeMarkets.

Retiring ten years out of business school has its benefits. Sam is able to focus on his family and instill his values in his kids. He is able to invest in others—literally—as they found and build their own startups. He has achieved independence that allows him to "beat the drum and march to his own beat," as he puts it. And although the ever-industrious Sam Kinney will never be truly retired, he enjoys the ability to choose his future, shape his own life, and focus on the relationships he cares so much about building.

Whit's Words

Fostering communication means building trust early with employees. Sam did this by rolling up his sleeves, working alongside people, and being willing to self-evaluate and encourage others to do the same. He also gained insight into his own leadership style and behaviors by opening himself up to evaluation. What better way to create transparency for self-improvement than to expose your strengths and weaknesses?

In order to build an environment of openness and safeness, you have to go down before you go up—you have to build a foundation before you can build a house. That involves trust. In the best-selling book *The Five Dysfunctions of a Team*, Patrick Lencioni shares his model to improve team effectiveness. It all begins with building trust amongst team members. Sam was a master at building trusting relationships so much that he was able to raise $500,000 in six days. His ability to prove his worth on the crew came through hard work, persistence, a sense of humor, and the ability to ask for and receive feedback and critique. It all began with trust.

If I were to interview your executive team and ask them to rate the degree of trust on your team and with their direct reports, what rating would they give? Without a foundation of trust, you will never produce the results you want out of your team. Sam produced results.

Here's an exercise you can use to build trust in your small team—it works best with four to eight people and takes about sixty minutes.

Exercise set up: Give everyone on your team a piece of flip chart paper and bring as many colored markers as you can find. You're going to give people five questions to answer, and they'll answer the questions by drawing, rather than speaking or writing their answers. They can't use words or numbers to answer the questions—they can only use pictures. Drawing forces people to access the creative side of their brain, while creating more introspective answers than when writing or speaking. Many people balk early on because they think they can't draw. Don't worry—as the facilitator/leader, draw an example for one of the questions to help ease them into the activity.

Give each member of the team fifteen minutes to draw their answers to the five questions.

1. What are your values, and who or what event helped shape those values?

2. If you could choose another career, what would it be, and why?

3. How do you deal with, or react to, conflict in interpersonal or group settings?

4. What advice would you give to your colleagues about working most effectively with you?

5. What was a significant challenge you faced as a child, and how does it influence you today?

After all have presented their drawing consider asking your team the following:

- What common themes did you hear?

- What is your reaction from what you've heard from your colleagues?

This exercise can help to break down some of the barriers of trust amongst your team members, but it is only a small step in the large task of building a high-performing team. Patrick Lencioni has four more steps to get to the top of his pyramid in pursuit of achieving high-level results. I highly recommend ordering the book for each member of your leadership team. Ask them to read the book and then hire an outside facilitator who is versed in Lencioni's work to take you and your team through each of the five stages.

Charlie Peterson

*Overcoming Fear by Focusing
Beyond Your Comfort Zone*

About Charlie

Charlie Peterson is an orthopedic surgeon specializing in shoulder surgery, joint reconstruction, and sports medicine. A fourth-generation surgeon in his family, he is the vice president and a seven-year board member of a $250-million-a-year company, Proliance Surgeons, a physician-owned-and-managed company with about 160 surgeons. He's also the past managing partner at Orthopedic Specialists of Seattle, a Proliance clinic on the forefront of orthopedic surgery and care. In 2011, he was voted one of the Top Doctors in Seattle by *Seattle Metropolitan Magazine*, an honor he was selected for out of nearly 4,000 nominees in three counties.

After graduating from Dartmouth magna cum laude with a BA in chemistry, Charlie earned his medical degree at the University of Washington. He went on to complete orthopedic residency training at the Mayo Clinic, one of the most prestigious orthopedic residency programs in the country. After completing residency, Charlie did a fellowship in sports medicine and shoulder surgery at the Hospital for Special Surgery in New York City. There, he was one of the assistant team doctors for the New York Mets and also worked occasionally with the New York Giants.

He met his wife, Nancy, during his freshman year at Dartmouth, where she also rowed, although they didn't start dating until their senior year. The two live in Seattle with their children, Sam and Gretchen. In his off time, he enjoys hiking, skiing, kayaking, sailing, and photography.

Getting to the Edge

Saying Charlie Peterson was thin as a high school senior is an understatement. At six feet, six inches tall and weighing around 150 pounds, he was a bit of a late bloomer. But while his height should have been an advantage, he never really excelled in anything sports-wise. He played basketball but was never a standout on his team. He was all height and no bulk, which wasn't a winning combination in the sport…or any other sports he'd tried, for that matter.

One evening, the summer before his freshman year at Dartmouth, Charlie was at an alumni picnic his parents were hosting. Across the room, he saw the woman who had conducted his college entrance interview, Annmarie. She was a friend of Martha Beattie (also a Peterson family friend), one of the first class of women rowers at Dartmouth and a star in the sport of crew. Annmarie crossed the room to talk to him, and as they were chatting, she suddenly said, "You know, you should really try out for crew when you get to Dartmouth. You would be awesome. The coaches would just drool over you at 150 pounds. You could be a national caliber lightweight!"

Flattered and a little embarrassed at the praise, he pondered the possibility of becoming a rower. While Charlie hadn't had much exposure to crew other than watching a University of Washington crew race or two in Seattle, the idea of competing in the sport intrigued him. He tucked the thought in the back of his mind, but still planned to pursue basketball once he arrived in Hanover. After all, he figured he was pretty good at basketball and certainly had height on his side.

Sadly, his hopes of playing basketball were quickly trampled the first few days at college. He made his way to the gym to meet the head coach and express interest in the team, only to be met with a clear look of disinterest. Still, the coach invited him to attend captain's practice, probably more out of politeness than genuine interest in Charlie as an athlete. But when he arrived at practice the next week, it became clear he wasn't even second-string level; if he were lucky, he'd be on the "C" squad, meaning he'd never play or go anywhere with basketball. While enjoying the game, Charlie never loved it enough to spend his college years riding the bench. So, remembering his conversation with Annmarie, he decided to walk down to the office of the head crew coach and introduce himself.

The coach looked at him, eyebrows bristling in an understated way, and said, "I think you'll be a heavyweight. Just show up at the docks."

Testing Limits

Charlie says, "If you are going to be successful at anything, unless you are gifted with incredible talent beyond that of most men, you're going to have to suffer and have travails, and you're going to have times when you are stretched to your limits in order to achieve your goals in that profession, be it business, law, medicine, or any other profession…. And you're going to have to be able to survive and thrive in order to meet your goals. In order to accomplish your goals, at some point in your life, you're going to have to be stretched, and you're going to have to be tested to know what your limits are—limits you think are there but actually really aren't once you get to that point. And you realize you can survive, and you can continue onward."

As he walked back across campus, Charlie saw a crew shell displayed on the Dartmouth Green, surrounded by some varsity rowers out recruiting new members. As Charlie walked by, his tall, lanky frame caught their attention. The athletes walked up and surrounded him and said, "You've got to come out and row." Charlie explained that he'd just talked to the head coach and was planning to come out, but they weren't having it. They dragged him down to the docks and got him started with the sport that very day.

His first practices with the freshman team of '86 were some of the best of Charlie's athletic life. Almost instantly, he realized he was a natural at the sport. Not only was he physically built to be a rower, he could become great at it simply through hard work. In the other sports he'd done, there always seemed to be a limit—no matter how hard he worked, his skill set dictated he could only be so good. There wasn't the same work–results relationship in crew. "It was an amazing thing for me to realize I could be really good at something athletic, and there was no limit as to what I could do," he says. "I wasn't the last guy chosen for the team or the skinniest guy on the basketball team or the guy who wasn't tall enough to be the center for the Dartmouth team. If I simply worked hard, I could be in the first boat and do really well at it." He quickly bonded with the rest of the team as they went through grueling workouts, pushing together to get past what they previously thought were their limitations. "There was a sense of camaraderie on the team that I had not experienced before," he adds. "We created that sense of a shared bond forged through suffering."

One particular drill had a great effect on Charlie, a drill that eventually became known in that immediate-post-Star Wars era as a "Darth Vader." The team would start at one river bridge and do a grueling, forty-five-minute row at about 80 percent power to another bridge. But there was a catch: it was also a seat race.

Seat racing in crew is used to determine the fastest eight men on the team to make up a winning boat. The objective of seat racing is to directly compare individuals, which is difficult to do on the water through any other method. There are numerous factors that go into putting together the fastest boat, including strength, height, weight, technique, ergometer scores, toughness, drive, and past experience. To conduct a seat race, the coach matches two oarsmen against one another in two different shells and puts together lineups for two roughly equal boats to race one another over a short distance. The boats start evenly as the race begins, and the coach times the race, measuring the distance between the winning and losing boat once the race is completed. He then switches one person from each boat and races again—and again and again—and may switch the same two oarsmen back and forth or switch other oarsmen so the race can't be rigged by those not involved in the seat race. Clever coaches never want the other oarsmen to know exactly who is being compared in each race—that way, they can ensure everyone is pulling hard for each race since anyone could be the subject of evaluation at any time.

That day in Tennessee was the first time the team had done two back-to-back forty-five-minute seat races. Late in those Darth Vaders, Charlie seemingly couldn't feel much of his body. His hands began bleeding because of reopening blisters he already had from earlier practices. But he kept rowing. Not only was he scared of losing a chance for a seat in the first boat, but he also had the immediate fear of getting whacked by one of the oars in front of him or behind him. Most of all, he feared letting down his teammates, something he did everything in his power to avoid.

The team never forgot that day of training, and we never did the drill again! Charlie's observation after that practice was, "Coach, there was nowhere to hide during those seat races." He realized he had to give 100 percent of himself 100 percent of the time.

"Those drills were brutal. I got to the point of pain where I was literally numb. But I'd finish them, I'd make it through, and I'd realize, 'I can do this,'" he recalls. "That kind of stretching was critical for me then, as well as in later parts of my life like residency. In residency, I was occasionally at the hospital almost all the time for a whole month. Some residents were so dogged tired that they literally didn't know what day it was. You end up bleary-eyed."

Train and Develop Willpower

Charlie recommends a book called Willpower: Rediscovering the Greatest Human Strength. *As he explains it, the book discusses scientists who studied willpower and found it's an actual, quantifiable thing in your body that you use up as you go through the day or through certain tasks. A lot of people who are the most successful in business, school, and other areas are able to focus their will to exert it in certain situations. The book also suggests that you can train and develop willpower like any other muscle in your body.* "Training in crew, training in that particular way where you put yourself through very harsh, rigorous conditions and come through on the other side, you have to focus your will," *he adds.* "I found that probably the most valuable thing I took away in terms of my career and life afterwards."

During his residency at the prestigious Mayo Clinic, Charlie would often be on for twenty-four-hour shifts, sleeping in the hospital, waking up to attend to patients. The hospital became his second home—or rather, his first home, during those rotations, at least. At times, he wondered how to carry on, but he looked back and remembered feeling similarly during those grueling drills his freshman year at Dartmouth. He knew limits are only limits until you surpass them—he could push further and harder, and he could get through the toughest hours of residency. And he could do so while giving his all and not failing those around him.

"I knew that no matter how bad it was, it wasn't as bad as the last bit of a Darth Vader," he explains. "I developed a degree of toughness I didn't know I had." Only this time, he didn't have to worry about getting whacked by an oar handle if he stopped pulling.

Along with perseverance, Charlie says freshman year of crew taught him valuable lessons about leadership that still carry with him today. "The key thing that worked really well for me, and I think for a lot of us in the boat, was that Whit respected us," he says. "He had a style that was persuasive, even occasionally demanding, yet low key and respectful, and still said, 'Look, I know you can do this; you don't know you can do this yet, but I know you can.'"

In his many roles—on the board of directors of Proliance Surgeons, as a managing partner of his care center, and while leading a surgical team—Charlie's leadership continues to be influenced by his days as a college athlete at Dartmouth. He quickly realized that screaming and ranting doesn't get effective results; what inspires those around him is pushing confidently and quietly, yet firmly, and showing respect to those around him. "I think, consciously or unconsciously, I try to emulate Whit's leadership coaching style," he says.

As the vice president of Proliance Surgeons, he has a unique challenge: leading other successful, strong-willed leaders. These top surgeons and doctors have strong opinions and personalities and are used to being in charge. The key to leading the group, he explains, is creating a strong buy-in by making sure everyone develops a powerful shared vision—rather than focusing on what they don't agree on. At his clinic and surgery center, he gives his employees opportunities to be in situations where they can succeed given the tools they have and a willingness to work hard. But the challenge, he says, is putting people in situations where they're not going to "slam dunk it," but also to not make it so hard that they're destined to fail. As a leader, one must learn to create situations that inspire and push the team to the edge of their limits, but never over the edge.

Perhaps the most poignant lesson that has carried with him into his work as a surgeon is the idea that self-confidence, self-control, and perseverance are keys to success. "No matter what walk of life you're in, from digging ditches to being president of the United States, at some point in your life you're going to be tested to your limits or close to them to have the measure of yourself to withstand challenges, whether they're physical, mental, or otherwise," he says. "For us in that boat in 1982, we reached that point."

Whit's Words

If you look back to Charlie's words, he says, "[The] challenge is putting people in situations where they're not going to 'slam dunk it,' but also to not make it so hard that they're destined to fail. As a leader, one must learn to create situations that inspire and push the team to the edge of their limits, but never over the edge."

I started working as a leadership coach in the early '80s when companies were sending their executive teams off site to ropes courses and outdoor team-building events. These Experiential Team Building activities took place in the woods, away from the familiarity of the office and city environments. I spent three years with top leaders from United Airlines, Kodak, and Mobil Oil, asking them to climb trees forty to sixty feet off the ground; use lumber, fifty-gallon barrels, and rope to build rafts strong enough to paddle across bodies of water; and walk across cable wires blindfolded while receiving coaching from teammates on the ground below. What was the purpose of these activities? What were we trying to do if, in fact, this was leadership development training?

The purpose was to put leaders into uncomfortable situations where they could only depend on their leadership skills in unfamiliar circumstances and give them scenarios where they had to solve problems without knowing the answers. They couldn't depend on their expertise or talents they had learned in business school.

Those "team building" events were a way of simulating fear, discomfort, and chaos, all the while asking for cooperation, collaboration, and leadership effectiveness. We found that people can learn a great deal through such experiences, hence the term, "experiential education," or learning by doing.

Charlie learned much about being uncomfortable and dealing with fear throughout his freshman rowing experience. He took those lessons, insights, and learning into the medical profession and has excelled as a teacher, physician, leader, and father.

As the leader of your team or organization, how do you take a group of professionals and help them overcome fear? How do you push them to the edge of their comfort zones, help them grow, and develop in their areas of expertise?

During the team building events, when we would hook up the executives to their climbing gear and explain the task of climbing the tree and walking across wires sixty feet up in the air, we would ask them to tell us how they would want to be coached through the climbing experience. We explained that we wanted them to push their learning—not to get to a place of panic. To do so, we asked each of them to evaluate the situation and tell us three things:

1. What would be your area of comfort where you could easily do the task?

2. What would be an area of learning? There might be fear, and you might push your level of comfort right to the edge. How would you like to be coached when you hit that edge or barrier in order to help you get past it?

3. What would put you in a panic zone? We don't want you in a panic zone, as the learning dramatically decreases.

Once we understood what the climber wanted to accomplish to "hit the edge and get uncomfortable," we would coach him or her to that place. Inevitably, people would get to where they had originally thought they would stop climbing and, through our positive coaching, recognize they had achieved their "edge" easier than they thought they could when they were looking at the course from the ground. With a little extra encouragement from the coach and a dose of courage, they would almost always surpass their original goals and push further.

Courage is the word that comes to mind as I think back to these experiences. In your own work each day, what would "courage" look like? Courage is the ability to face adversity and have enough confidence in your abilities and the relationships you've built over time to do the right thing. It takes courage to give your boss feedback about his/her behavior and the impact that behavior has on you and even more courage to ask for feedback. It takes courage to ask a colleague to change the way they think and work with you. It takes courage to step forward and pronounce your ideas in a meeting of experts. It takes courage to listen and not be the first one to always speak up. It takes courage to admit when you're wrong in front of your boss and colleagues. I think that courage is the prerequisite for confidence, and we could all use a little more self-confidence.

For employees to feel your investment in their success, you must be willing to help them set goals that are achievable, with some goals on their edge of their comfort zone, and then help, support, and en–*courage* them to reach those goals. If you do so, you will have employees with higher motivation, engagement, and courage to achieve superior results. Help them see their own capabilities and coach them with kind words and gentle pushing from behind. Then watch the success begin.

Sam Hartwell

*Investing in People
Before You Know the Result*

About Sam

Sam Hartwell joined KickStart International in 2007 as CFO and has since worked toward a grand vision: ending poverty in Africa. This not-for-profit social enterprise accomplishes its mission in a surprisingly commercial manner "by designing, manufacturing, and mass-marketing affordable tools millions of poor people can buy and use to create highly profitable businesses and take their first major step out of poverty."* When KickStart recruited Sam, sixteen prior years of growth had pushed the organization's infrastructure beyond its limits. Most worrying was the risk of fraud invading parts of Africa, which contributed to these areas being some of the most challenging places in the world to do business. Sam's job was to move to Nairobi, take control of the finances, and strengthen business systems. The challenges were formidable. First, Sam had to overcome major cultural differences as an American leading a team of thirty Africans. Then, almost immediately upon arriving with his family, Kenya's disputed presidential election triggered an explosion of violence that killed more than 1,500 innocent citizens and displaced 200,000 more.

Sam's two decades of work experience in for-profit and not-for-profit sectors were ideally suited to the job of overhauling KickStart's finances, which included a comprehensive enterprise software implementation, a monumental undertaking under normal circumstances, but a landmark achievement in KickStart's remote areas of operation. This involved building an IT infrastructure between the United States and four African countries with unreliable connectivity. Sam also took on the role of heading KickStart's metrics unit and launching a groundbreaking evaluation of KickStart's social impacts. These robust systems, measurements, and controls proved essential to KickStart's

---

*"About KickStart," *KickStart*, http://www.kickstart.org/about-us/.

continued growth—17 percent per year during Sam's first four years of tenure. As of February 2013, the organization had helped 750,000 people out of poverty and created 150,000 new businesses that generate over $120 million a year in net incomes and wages. KickStart's CEO, Martin Fisher, credits much of the organization's recent success to Sam and his team. For their transformative results, Sam was selected as a 2012 finalist for the San Francisco Bay Area CFO of the Year Awards.

Sam returned to the United States in 2010 to work from KickStart's headquarters. He has now joined Propeller Industries in San Francisco, where he provides outsourced CFO support to KickStart and early-stage companies. He has an MBA from Yale University and a BA from Dartmouth. When he's not in the office, he can be found in close proximity to his wife, Jennifer, and two children, Ben and Mae, whom he frequently wrangles into outdoor adventures.

A Story of Epic Proportions

Sam has always believed in the importance of working toward a grand vision of the future. He explains that inside each person is a desire—a need—to identify and strive for a story of epic proportions. Whether that story is winning a race, launching a new company, or creating thousands of jobs throughout a region of the world, the critical element is working with others to achieve something greater than what they might do alone. Sam helps others recognize that these stories are rarely, if ever, autonomous achievements. It takes many motivated individuals to accomplish a shared vision. When members of a group are able to bring intensity and focus to reach the goal, they become a team. Only then can they achieve greatness. "Epic accomplishments are always much bigger than any one person; this helps to unify the team. The trick is creating a shared vision that will sustain the team over the long journey to success. For example, at KickStart, we wanted to create the best finance functions, under the most difficult business conditions, with the least resources," Sam explains. "I asked my team, 'How many of you have created the best finance functions before?' The implication was we all—including me—had something to learn, and we would need to figure this out together."

Sam began developing his understanding of teamwork and leadership during his freshman crew experience at Dartmouth. He gained instant credibility with the group for the knowledge he brought from Salisbury School in northwest Connecticut, where he had been the crew's co-captain and had the great fortune to have rowed internationally as a high school athlete. Coming off a summer of building trails in the White Mountains, Sam came to Dartmouth in excellent physical condition. Throughout his college career, he consistently put up faster erg times than much heavier oarsmen. Over the course of the season, as teammates vied for seats in the first boat, they recognized something else about him: no matter who else was in the boat, Sam brought his full effort to that team. Early on, his example and unassuming, good humor motivated others to work harder, while helping to create a fierce work ethic with a strong sense of camaraderie.

As the year progressed, the team bond grew stronger. Each member began to recognize the individual talent and contributions they brought to the group. Some exemplified hard work, while others showed up with natural given talent. Some possessed mental focus, while others had physical prowess. As they began to recognize these strengths and accept each other's weaknesses, the young men who joined this freshman crew—many with a shrug of a shoulder and a "why not" attitude—became more than individuals. They became a team. "I suppose what tied us together was our mutual respect for each other and that we were all dedicated to putting extreme effort into our training and racing outcome. In the beginning, we didn't know what we were capable of since we were committing to achieving unprecedented goals. But Whit brought us together and said, 'If you do the training and work as a team, you can beat the other crews on our schedule.'" Sam explains, "That's the beauty of an epic; it's a shared experience in which each person pushes his limits and finds inspiration from others doing the same. Working together, the team becomes greater than the sum of its parts."

To the uninitiated, rowing may look like a contest of individual strength and endurance. What's easy to miss is that it's literally a tightrope act; put an empty shell on the water and it will invariably list to port or starboard. While muscle and drive can win a race, they are worth little if the boat pitches to one side. On the recovery, oars meant to be off the water will scrape along its surface, squandering hard-won momentum. During the stroke, blades will wash out at the finish when they ought to be buried, while pushing water towards the stern. "Keeping a boat 'set' while 1,600 pounds of meat is sliding around on deck requires the collective awareness of a Buddhist monastery," says Sam. "You have eight men who want nothing more than to win a race—who must recruit every muscle fiber in their own bodies—but who also have to keep precise timing with the others, no matter the strain." It can be elusive, but when you're in the zone, power is transferred to hull speed with seemingly perfect efficiency. With each stroke, the boat leaps from the water and you bury your opponent. For a coach or coxswain, it's magnificent to behold—eight highly conditioned athletes, under tremendous exertion, working together as a team in perfect harmony.

Even these many years later, Sam underplays the influence he had on the class of '86 Dartmouth freshman crew. But as his coach, I was able to see the way his teammates looked to him for inspiration and guidance. On race days, Sam didn't get overly excited or pumped up, but rather stayed quiet to allow his mind to focus on the race. When he did speak, it was with great intention, as though he was guarding some dormant inner flame he would spark only during the race—an intense desire for his team to row their best, come what may. His focus was contagious, helping center the team on the goal of the day. "Commitment is like sincerity; once you can fake *that*, you've got it made," Sam jokes. "All kidding aside, you're either focused and bring intensity to the race or you're not, but it's something everybody in the boat can feel immediately. I believe that if you bring total commitment to your work, you may inspire others to do the same."

Decades later, Sam was able to use the intensity and focus from his Dartmouth days as he embarked on a truly epic story: eliminating poverty in Africa, or at least giving his all toward that mission. After spending many years building finances and operations in nonstandard assignments, including in a public company with more than a billion dollars in sales, a turnaround in green tech, and venture-backed start-ups, Sam applied to become CFO at KickStart International. He was compelled by the founders' irreverence for charitable efforts that simply *feel* good and their all-out commitment to do *real* good by engineering measurable and lasting solutions to the world's biggest problems. KickStart's ambition is to eradicate poverty by creating money-making opportunities in the most economically challenged areas of the world. Sure, working on such a large-scale project was daunting, but Sam believed a committed team could make a big difference and that his for-profit experience might help.

After days of waiting for word on the position, Sam finally received an e-mail from the leadership of KickStart. He opened it with anticipation and read a surprising message: "We've decided to move this position to Nairobi. If you're still interested, please let us know." With a seven-year-old son, a five-year-old daughter, and a wife with a full tenure-track position at a university, Sam knew he couldn't expect his family to pack up and head to Africa. He arrived at home that evening, having mostly decided against the idea, and casually mentioned the e-mail to his wife. He was surprised when Jennifer looked at him, her face full of excitement, and said, "Sam, we've *got* to do this! This is the most incredible opportunity, to go overseas and live in Kenya." It was clear her mind was set; she was willing to take the risk and, perhaps more than he, understood the significance this event could have in their family's lives. Their kids were ecstatic at the prospect of moving to Africa, a continent they had studied in school. Soon, the Hartwell family had sold their house in West Hartford to move across the world.

As he developed and led the team at KickStart, Sam reflected that much of what he had learned from crew would be useful in his new position as CFO of this global organization. There was a huge task ahead of him. The organization was a year behind on its annual audits; accounting systems were disconnected and unsupervised, opening the company up for errors, inaccuracies, and theft; and inventory management and receivables needed serious attention. These were pervasive structural problems that would require commitment from the entire 250-person organization to solve. Sam would need to articulate his vision of positive change, get into the trenches with his team, and seek out and encourage elite performers. He knew leading this change as a foreigner would be especially difficult, and more so given the atmosphere of hopelessness and loss that had followed Kenya's postelection violence.

The cultural barriers became obvious as he worked alongside one of the most promising members of his team, Peter Juma, a native of Kenya. Living in a developing nation full of racial tension both within the country and between westerners and Kenyans, Peter never imagined he'd be working on the same projects, while having equal responsibilities as "wazungu" like Sam. "What really astonished this guy was I didn't treat him differently than an expatriate. It was easy for me—but to him, my lack of prejudice was a singularity," Sam explains. Growing up as a black African in a former British colony, where tribalism and bigotry have been legitimized and even encouraged, Peter's antenna was attuned to even the subtlest disparity in social hierarchy—and he was continually amazed he could not pick up these signals from Sam.

During their first meeting together, Sam and Peter created a shared story, a vision and mission that would drive their work and inspire them during challenging times. Together, they decided they would build the best finance department in their sector—a goal not easily reached, considering KickStart's current state. By doing so, they would complete a journey together and help put the organization in a position to expand its operations and change the lives of hundreds of thousands of families. Although they spent their first year working separately, the second year, Sam promoted Peter to join the headquarter team and later made him the controller for the whole KickStart organization. Over the three-and-a-half years Sam was in Africa, their work relationship developed into a friendship, and Sam became a mentor to Peter. "We engaged on a fundamental level, just like two people on a crew would, which is, 'If you bring your all, and I bring mine, we *can* achieve this goal,'" Sam explains. "We knew there was an opportunity before us to do something great."

Often, the times make the men—and these were no exceptions. Under Sam's direction and leadership, KickStart's finances were integrated into one department. An internal auditing system was put into place, and stricter accounting practices helped improve accuracy and reduce fraud and theft. Receivables were collected 40 percent faster. The organization expanded its retail network to over 450 stores across four countries and began shipping pumps—irrigation tools that allow farmers to create sustainable, profitable farms—to over twenty-three countries in Africa and around the world. But most significantly, Sam and Peter's story was realized. KickStart had achieved the most comprehensive enterprise resource planning (ERP) system implementation of its type in Africa, putting it in the best position possible to expand and further its mission.

One day, after they'd been working together for some time, Peter sent a letter to Sam. In it, he detailed the profound impact Sam had on his life. It remains one of the most moving letters Sam has ever received from an employee, which he treasures not just for its appreciative words, but for Peter's account of his own fears and leap of faith. Excerpts show the unique relationship the two had formed, as well as the positive influence Sam had on Peter's life:

> What I know is that you are a great person, leader, manager, and friend. And as I have always said, you are different. You look at things differently, with a wider perspective... .
>
> In April of 2008, when you approached me to take up a position in the Africa office, it marked yet another milestone in my career. Again, against any odds, I saw in you a person who believed in people for what they have and not what they are. And when I raised my fears about how I was going to fit in a totally new role in the organization structure, you promised and stood with me in educating everybody that cared to listen about what I can do. You believed in me. You told me I was capable. You gave me hope. You increased my confidence. I have actually done and accomplished things that even amaze me. I just can't imagine how much people can do if given the opportunity... .

I will forever be grateful for having had the opportunity to work with such a great person like you. You have been such an inspiration. I want to let you know that I really appreciate the hard work you have been doing to try and make people understand my role and make my work easier. This is something I will forever be grateful for.

Thank you so much and much appreciated.

Peter

This note of recognition helped confirm for Sam his leadership philosophy throughout the companies and cultures he had helped create: identify a story of epic proportions, devote yourself fullheartedly as a team member, and invest in others before you know the result. And while Sam and Peter never could have guessed the synergy they would reach, both personally and professionally, they had been willing to take the risk—and it has paid off for both of them. "Peter could work almost anywhere, but he has stayed at KickStart because of how he's treated, and we are enormously lucky to have him," says Sam. "In truth, we never could have accomplished so much without Peter and his readiness to trust me and the other senior leaders at KickStart."

While his mentorship with Peter was a big part of Sam's life in Africa, he felt privileged to work with the entire KickStart team. "The best part of living out an amazing adventure is reaping its intrinsic rewards. When a team accomplishes something very hard, the sense of achievement is incentive enough. There was a time when you were not even sure it was possible—and now, by working together, you've done it! It's a realization that needs no recognition; it's intoxicating enough that you and your team know you did something few others could. The experience can make you a believer in the old saw, that anything in life truly worth doing is difficult—because if it were not, everyone would be doing it."

Sam likens management to crew: "Managers need to recognize that people will bring different strengths and weaknesses, and it's their job to continually reconfigure roles in ways that maximizes the team's collective abilities. If you create a culture and work environment that allows people to connect to each other and apply themselves positively toward reaching their full potential, then it's part of human nature to want to deliver complete commitment to that—this is what Whit helped us understand at an early age."

Recognizing the epic is just the first step toward greatness and, for Sam, that vision must be accompanied by follow-through and committing to others before knowing the result of the investment. In his own way, this is how Sam led at Dartmouth and in Africa: by working wholeheartedly alongside anyone he could rouse to the challenge of an epic adventure.

Value from Everyone

"I see a lot of young professionals, particularly Americans, who are somewhat disappointed with the jobs available to them when they get out of school," Sam explains. *"They have great expectations of what their education should enable them to do. My advice: assume you can learn something from everyone—a receptionist, a shipping clerk, a plant manager—anybody. If you make the most of all relationships, you'll find the opportunities to add value are everywhere."*

Whit's Words

How do you know who to invest in, especially when the future is unknown? Where can the right individuals fit into your organization? Where can they add the most value to the team? How can you match a person's strengths and skills with both what the job requires today and the growth and future of your company? Most of the time, people will live up to your expectations when you share conviction and commitment with them.

Exceptional leaders like Sam and Peter can often see a person's potential more clearly than the person can see it. If members of your team are having trouble seeing their potential, you can help:

- Develop a set of questions that will evaluate whether a new job or opportunity will play to their strengths.

- Give them courage to try something new or challenging they wouldn't try without your encouragement.

- Direct them away from trying to be something they are not.

Start with their strengths. What can you do to exploit what they are already great at doing? If you can create the right conditions and opportunities for your employees to master and increase the effectiveness of their greatest strengths by 10 to 15 percent, you'll reap terrific rewards throughout your organization. Yes, we all have blind spots that need some attention, but your results will be far greater if you capitalize on their strengths. When you invest early in people's potential and work together to identify strengths and a shared vision, you give them the best chance for success.

Consider these questions as you think about investing in others before you know their full potential:

1. How can you coach your high-potential, upcoming leaders around maximizing their strengths and neutralizing their weaknesses?

2. Have you found yourself encouraging your direct reports to look for what their employees are doing well?

3. How have you praised your direct reports for their progress? What encouragement have you given them to continue to change and grow?

4. Are you able to see the potential in others before they see it themselves? What can you do with those insights?

5. Do they see their better selves through your words, commitment, and actions?

Remember this: "Great leaders inspire people to make commitments they wouldn't otherwise make." Be the person to inspire change and growth in those around you.

Dan Kollmorgen

Transformation in Leadership through Team Input

About Dan

Dan Kollmorgen is a surgical oncologist and physician leader at The Iowa Clinic, the largest physician-owned multispecialty clinic in Iowa. His roles have included positions on the Board of Directors, Patient Care Committee, and Marketing Committee. At Iowa Methodist Medical Center, he is the chairman of surgery, director of the Stoddard Cancer Center, and member of the Surgical Residency faculty. Dan has been honored as teacher of the year for the residency program multiple times, was named Physician of the Year at The Iowa Clinic, and serves on the Commission on Cancer for The American College of Surgeons. His focus as a surgeon is not only on saving the lives of his patients, but also advancing the future of medicine by improving the quality and value of complex cancer care.

Dan graduated magna cum laude with a major from Dartmouth in biology and went on to complete his MD at the University of Iowa, College of Medicine. He did his surgical residency at the University of Utah and cancer fellowship at Roswell Park Cancer Institute in New York. He lives in Des Moines, Iowa, with his wife, Karen, and their two children, Kellen and Anna. When he's not working, he enjoys exercise, outdoor sports, and family time.

A 360° Look at Leadership

Dan was recruited to play football at Dartmouth. As a teenager, he'd been a star athlete, and he expected the same in college. But plans have a way of changing, especially when you're eighteen years old, fearless, and willing to try anything.

As Dan went through practice and play during that first season of Dartmouth football, he realized that he was outgrowing the sport. What used to excite him—the crowds, the energy of the team—

began to feel too familiar and comfortable. He thought back to what his parents had told him as he was preparing to leave for school: "You've got four years to be selfish and do the best you can to make yourself as good as you can. This is an incredible opportunity—it's our gift to you. Take those four years, but after that you've got to start giving back." He'd promised them that his focus would be on reinventing himself, trying new challenges, while taking advantage of his time in college. It was time to start.

Malcolm McIver, Dan's roommate his freshman year at Dartmouth, encouraged Dan to join crew. As he watched Malcolm go through fall practice and saw the unity and bond within the team, along with the subtle, yet dynamic, movements of crew, Dan became more and more interested in the sport. "This is one of the things that I wanted, to try different activities. It seemed like rowing was a combination of dynamic strength, aerobic fortitude, and mental endurance," he explains. "It was appealing on a number of levels." There was something about the rowing team that intrigued this tight end from Iowa—it gave him a new opportunity to push beyond his limits in a way he hadn't previously experienced. As he saw Malcolm and the other members of the team push themselves physically and mentally, he was drawn to the focused dedication required of this special freshman class of '86.

January of their freshman year came quickly, and all returned from Christmas break, knowing ahead of time that the winter workouts would test their limits. They had been sent home with daily workouts and an accountability training sheet to complete. What a wonderful surprise for me when Dan walked into the tank room with Malcolm. Here was a football player from Iowa who stood six feet four inches and over 200 pounds. Knowing enough about football, I was confident he could handle the intensity and workouts I would require over the long winter months in Hanover.

Dartmouth is one of the northernmost colleges in the country, so the ice from the long winters doesn't leave the river until mid-March. Time on the water is essential for speed early in the season, and the collegiate rowing teams in Boston were able to get on the water one month earlier since the ice melted faster two hours south of Hanover. Because of the lack of access to water, we relied on the indoor rowing tanks, cross country skiing, weight lifting, and long runs to help condition the athletes in preparation for the spring racing season. All of those workouts made for a very long training season.

Dan, who had no previous experience in crew, pretty much did whatever I told him to do. Dan was a quiet but very powerful force, and I could tell he was going to contribute to the speed of the team. His drawback was he had not learned the technique of rowing in the previous fall season, and I knew that would affect his ability to get into the first freshman boat. He hadn't developed the skill of getting the oar in and out of the water while sitting in a very skinny and tippy shell. But this challenge didn't alter his willingness and pure dedication to work his tail off all winter.

"I thought my sheer strength would balance out my inexperience, but I quickly learned that it's not strength that makes a great rower—it's the *way* that strength is used. I wasn't necessarily channeling my strength," Dan says. "I had to learn balance and a feel for the boat." He had to work to catch up with the team and learn the art of rowing. But the challenge was just what he'd hoped for, and he was fulfilling just what his parents had encouraged him to do in trying new opportunities.

Dan found that crew and football were more different than he'd originally realized. While both were team sports, crew had a very personal and individual element to it. Each athlete had to train hard and perform well for the team to be successful, and the boat was only as strong as the weakest athlete. After all, a football team can score a touchdown if one player is underperforming, but a crew can't win a race without all members performing at their highest levels. Each rower must build his strength and skill, while learning to work with the team as a whole. "As a crew, you have to find that rhythm, find that swing. Sometimes it takes more individual work, and sometimes it takes more team practice," Dan explains.

The immediate feedback from crew was also new to Dan. While training on the rowing ergometers or racing, he was able to instantly see the results of his work, unlike football, which was adjusted in the moment as a reaction to the game. He valued seeing the outcome quickly and being able to train to improve. This would serve him well in his later career as a surgeon, where the results are just as immediate—either a patient gets well or doesn't. Time management also became important to Dan as he balanced yearlong workouts with academics, which barely left time for a social life. He learned to be efficient and prioritize his time. And finally, the strong, family-like bond he made with his rowing mates was unlike anything he'd experienced in football. The shared experiences with the team—travel, practices, races, and dinners together—became an integral part of his college experience. Sitting in a shell with eight other teammates, two or more hours each day for nine months, was different from any team experience he had been through growing up around the cornfields and football fields of Iowa.

In his effort to reinvent himself, Dan was unexpectedly transformed from a football hero into a quiet leader. He found that he didn't have to be a star vying for attention. "I don't think the guys on the team were looking for a loud, boisterous, charismatic person; they were looking for someone who was organized, had vision, and enabled others," Dan says. "As a bowman in the four-oared shell that went to the Henley Royal Regatta my senior year at Dartmouth, I learned that I didn't have to be in the stroke seat to provide leadership and be a vital member. I learned that I could help the team without having to get all the credit." As he went through those four years rediscovering who he was in this new environment, he learned that crew was right in line with his values: it taught him a natural way to lead. "The further along I get in life, the more I realize that leaders aren't the guys who grab the slack and run forward; they're the ones who are the listeners, the problem solvers, the ones who help people achieve what they want to achieve in the bigger sense," he adds.

Unlike many other sports, crew doesn't have an award at the end of the year for most valuable player. But there are leaders on all crews. The key leader on any championship crew may not be the biggest, strongest, toughest, meanest guy in the boat. Instead, leaders usually come out as the oarsmen who understand team dynamics. They are the ones who know when to speak up before or after races. They are the guys who take the lead when the coach isn't around and gain the respect of the others based on their words and actions.

Little did Dan know, his days of reinventing himself were not over when he graduated from college and, later, medical school—and his education in leadership wasn't finished either. In his position as a lead surgical oncologist working in the surgical residency program at The Iowa Clinic, he thought that his leadership style was working. Lives were being saved, resident surgeons were being properly trained, and complex cancer cases were being given the utmost care and attention. He was working with great residents, several of whom were college athletes or had a military background, since he knew that they had the staying power and drive to handle surgery. His section of the clinic flourished, and he was able to go to sleep at night with a clear head and conscience, knowing he'd done the most he could do medically for the patients in his care. However, he didn't realize there was a part of his leadership behavior that needed a major overhaul.

Recognizing the major changes on the horizon in health care, The Iowa Clinic started a Leadership Training Institute in conjunction with the University of South Florida. Based on his experience and position in the Clinic, Dan was strongly encouraged to attend. With thoughts like, "I don't have time for this," and "I'm *already* a leader," he begrudgingly attended the course, eager for the minutes to pass so he could get back on the surgical floor. In the class, all executives and physicians were asked to complete a 360 evaluation, a process which elicits feedback from colleagues, peers, direct reports, and bosses. Dan had to choose people within his circle of influence and impact and went through the motions of the evaluation, not expecting much to come of it. But when he received the objective data and subjective comments from his circle of twenty raters, he was shocked to read a good amount of negative feedback. He couldn't help but wonder, "What am I doing wrong?"

"It was a wakeup call—I'd never looked in the mirror before or listened to the subtle feedback," Dan reflects. "The main learning tool I took away from the evaluation was my lack of self-awareness, not only in how I learned, how I led, and what options there were in leadership, but realizing I could take time to reflect, think about what I'm doing, and recognize my strengths and weaknesses. Everybody saw me from a different angle, and it was very different from how I had perceived myself, so it was eye-opening for me." After the completion of his work in the program and based on the "blind spots" uncovered from the 360 evaluation, Dan's leadership behaviors made significant changes in his work with others throughout the organization and even at home.

Three Lessons for Young Leaders

Now that he's on the other side of the leadership course, Dan has three lessons he can offer young leaders. First, be self-aware of your "brand," what you stand for and represent. Know why you get out of bed every day and what you bring to a given situation. Second, embrace shared experiences, and enjoy the process of building camaraderie with those around you. Enjoy the transition into something new, whether it's from football, crew, or another passion. Third, value relationships. People respond to those with whom they have a relationship, not someone who dictates to them what to do.

One of the first points he realized was the behavior he displayed as a physician in the operating room didn't translate well into developing positive and effective personal and professional relationships. In the operating room, there isn't time for negotiation or consensus—a life is on the line and a decision must be made, and fast. But outside of the OR, Dan found it important to learn to slow down and be considerate of people. "The Leadership Institute at The Iowa Clinic really helped me recognize how important it is to take a little time for yourself, using that time for reflection," he explains. "It's okay to smile and enable other people. Through my mentorship in the leadership class, I learned the soft approach is hard for me—the compliments, the relationships, taking the time to really listen and put down my phone, to stop trying to text, e-mail, talk to my nurse, and teach residents all at once. The most valuable asset I have is my time. People will blossom and respond if I purposefully make time to listen and understand."

Dan's main focus in revamping his leadership was learning to listen—*really* listen. He learned to be softer in his approach, less blunt and direct. In many ways, the class brought him back to the leadership qualities he learned in crew—to be a quiet leader, leading from the bow seat through his support, attention, and a more sensitive approach to leadership. And these qualities translated to home, too, where he has learned to be more attentive to his family. After all, he realized, kids grow up so fast, and he wants to be a part of their growth. The "new" Dan sees life as all about relationships.

Like all leaders, Dan's leadership is still a work in progress, and he's the first to admit that he doesn't have it all figured out. "I don't want to leave the impression that I'm a polished and accomplished leader," he says. "I struggle every day with personal relationships, impatience, and poor listening, among other traits. I hope my message is about the ongoing journey of leadership, rather than arrival at the position." With statements like that, it's clear why he's now so deeply respected at the clinic—both by his patients and those he leads.

Whit's Words

Wouldn't you love to work in an environment where it is safe to go out and ask for feedback on your leadership style and behaviors? If this sounds a bit scary, think how scary it must be for the people who work for you and with you to share their keen insights if you don't make it safe for them to do so.

We all have blind spots in how we behave and work with others. How many of us feel safe enough to tell each other what those blind spots are or how they alter the relationship? In my executive coaching, I use instruments that allow others to provide needed feedback, tips, and ideas on what a person is doing well and what could be done better. The comments and ratings are anonymous, allowing people to feel comfortable completing the evaluation without fear of retribution. Dan experienced one such evaluation—a 360-degree review—that "woke him up" to his behaviors and the impact his actions were having on his colleagues.

Shock, anger, rejection, and acceptance are likely the four emotions Dan went through after receiving his 360-degree feedback data. These are typical reactions that come from successful people upon discovering they're not perfect—or that others don't see them as near-perfect leaders. Often, a person's first thought is to find out who said such "awful" comments about them. The second thought is to figure out ways to disclaim what was said about them. The third thought is to reject this 360-degree process and not deal with any of the valuable feedback it provides. But with the support of coaching, self-observation, and reflection, most people usually get to some sense of acceptance and then begin the change process.

Many clients often ask how to best utilize the feedback in the 360-degree review. The people who filled out the evaluations want to know that their comments were heard and considered. If nothing changes, you are unlikely to ever receive open and honest feedback again. You have lots of data on many different areas of your leadership behaviors and abilities. Do you try to change everything? The answer is no! Here are some tips on what to do to make 360 evaluations effective:

1. Recognize that one comment may not represent the truth for you or others. Decide which of the comments need your attention and more investigation. Let the other comments go.

2. Look for common themes in the feedback—not just negative feedback. What did your raters say about your strengths? What positive influence have you had on others in your organization? Were you aware of these positive behaviors and the impact you have had on others?

3. Review the statements that you may not understand. Ask questions of those who completed the instrument to clarify any confusing statements.

4. Remember to thank those raters who took the time to complete your evaluation for their comments and insights.

5. Even if everyone on your team didn't participate in the 360 evaluations, it is your duty to share the feedback you received. Pick one behavior that you have decided to change and improve upon. Announce to your team the actions you will take to master this chosen behavior.

6. Tell your team that over the next three months, you will be asking for input and direct feedback to ensure change occurs.

Throughout this process, you will create a new culture of feedback where people will be encouraged to ask for and be willing to give and receive feedback from each other as a way to take their growth and development to a higher level. Many people have the mentality of, "Change is great, but you go first." If you, their leader, decide that you want change and transformation in your culture, you need to go first.

Mark Proctor

*Personal Responsibility
through Care for People*

About Mark Proctor

Mark Proctor is a neurosurgeon and head of the Brain Injury Center at Boston Children's Hospital, as well as a specialist and international leader in skull deformities, a field he is helping shape in new and exciting ways. As the director of residency training at Boston Children's Hospital, he trains the next generation of pediatric neurosurgeons, and his role on the admissions committee at Harvard Medical School means he helps select tomorrow's physicians and leaders in medicine. He's also president-elect of the Physicians' Organization of Children's Hospital, past-chairman of the ThinkFirst National Injury Prevention Foundation, secretary and upcoming chairman of the Pediatric Section of the American Association of Neurological Surgeons, as well as the 2009 recipient of the Distinguished Service Award from the Congress of National Neurosurgeons for work in injury prevention.

But Mark is more than just a title and accolades—he is a physician known for his exceptionally high level of patient care, a teacher who works tirelessly to train new doctors, and a father who rejoices in his kids' successes. He is a surgeon who stays in the operating room throughout every procedure, rather than merely stepping in at crucial moments and allowing residents to do the rest of the work. He's able to recall patients with surprising detail and feels a strong sense of personal responsibility for each and every life.

Mark received his BA in French from Dartmouth and his MD from Columbia University, one of the top schools in the country. He lives with his wife, Charlotte, and children, Max and Kenny, in Newton, Massachusetts. When he isn't saving lives, he enjoys playing squash and cycling.

From Academic to Athlete to World-Class Surgeon

In high school, Mark was known for being smart. It was how he saw himself and how others viewed him as well. He was at the top of his class, on the honor roll, and involved in leadership with service organizations. Academics came easily to him—it was a part of his identity, and it brought respect.

But this intellectual world Mark thrived in was solitary. It involved hard work by himself and for himself. While he enjoyed academics, it didn't give him the chance to connect with others, and he certainly wasn't pushing himself physically. Since he saw himself as a scholar, he never thought he'd be a part of a team, let alone a sports team. Of course, life sometimes takes a different direction than people think it will, and Mark's life was no exception.

Like many of the young men on the freshman crew at Dartmouth, Mark was first attracted to the sport by seeing the crew shell sitting on the Dartmouth Green. He'd never seen a shell before, let alone a rowing race, and he curiously walked by, wondering why the boat was sitting out. Luckily, one of the recruiters saw something in Mark that he didn't. At six feet three inches and with the lean build of a rower, he was a natural fit for the sport. Although he'd never given sports a second thought, he decided to try it out, to see if he could push himself in athletics the way he'd pushed himself in academics. If nothing else, he'd give it a good go.

Mark quickly learned that crew fit him perfectly. "I can't even imagine what my college career would've been like if it weren't for rowing," Mark says. "It was the defining part of my college life." As he forced himself out of bed for those early morning practices and pushed through the fatigue of long, intense workouts, he found two new sides to himself: an athlete and a teammate. But it was more than

174

that. Mark's self-perception began to change as his body became stronger; he was no longer just an academic—he was an athlete. Strenuous workouts gave him a rush, and his physical confidence grew. Although he had to work hard to keep up with his teammates, a couple of whom had rowed in high school before coming to Dartmouth and most of whom had done a sport in high school, he didn't care. His muscles began to tone and he didn't tire as easily. His body began to learn the motions of rowing, and the movements started to feel natural to him, as though his body had been waiting to be trained in the sport. That's when Mark realized a profound self-discovery: he could accomplish anything he wanted to, if he put in the work.

I remember Mark as a quiet guy who seemed awkward in his own body. He recognized that he was not going to be the best athlete in crew, but he kept coming back time and time again. He would show up early for practice and wait patiently for the boat positions to be posted. Mark occasionally ended up sitting in the launch with me or was sent off for a run because we had too many oarsmen during the fall practice sessions, and he wasn't one of the better skilled oarsmen in the top sixteen. I would put him into the shell at some point during practice to give him a go at it. He never became discouraged and, in fact, continued to push himself day in and day out. Mark never complained; he just kept coming back down to the boathouse because he wanted to row. When he made it into the second boat for spring season, it was accomplished through persistence and showing me he wasn't going to give up. I recognized those qualities in him.

I later learned Mark had continued to row all four years, and his junior year he won the Most Improved Heavyweight Oarsman award from the famous head Dartmouth men's rowing coach, Peter Gardner. When asked about the award, Mark says he thinks

Pete gave it to him because he showed up every morning during the winter workouts when others had slept in. He was persistent and, in his quiet way, never willing to give in. On my team and throughout his time in crew, he kept up the same level of commitment and personal responsibility. And while those qualities existed before crew, the sport gave him an opportunity to apply those qualities outside of academics and develop a side of himself he may not have had the chance to develop. Of course, he began to see himself differently, too—as an athlete and someone who could accomplish whatever he set out to do.

Crew did more than just help reshape his identity and self-perception; it also positively influenced his medical school applications and his subsequent training to become a brain surgeon. Although Mark applied to many schools around the country, he had his heart set on Columbia University College of Physicians and Surgeons, a school consistently ranked among the top in the country. He knew his chances were slim, as only around 4.5 percent of candidates are accepted to the prestigious institution each year. When his acceptance letter came in the mail on the day the team left for spring training in Tennessee, Mark was both elated and shocked. Recalling the Columbia entrance interview, he remembered the interviewer talking about the prestigious medical school rugby team, and he realized his athletic background may have been what got him the coveted acceptance; Columbia wanted another rugby player. Since they knew he was a former crew athlete, they assumed Mark could make the transition to play rugby. "Crew didn't influence my decision to go into medicine," Mark explains. "But I am absolutely certain it influenced where I went to medical school. I got into a much better school than I would have gotten into based on my academics alone." Being a part of crew gave him a standout résumé, making him a unique candidate and giving him the chance to train at one of the best schools possible.

As he entered the grueling world of medical school and residency—in which sleep was rare and tiredness seemed to permeate every aspect of daily life—Mark drew on his crew training. Many nights and early mornings, he dragged himself out of bed to perform the mechanical, methodical movements of surgery. As he did this day after day, month after month, he began to see parallels to crew—the early mornings on the Connecticut River, his body doing the same motions over and over again, pushing through the tiredness and fatigue to get his body to perform at its highest level. Those long hours spent rowing were perfect training for surgery, and he was able to draw from his time during crew to summon the determination he'd found on the water. His body remembered its ability to push through pain and exhaustion, and he was able to do the same for his patients. He was able to give his best, even if he didn't feel in top form, and he knew he was capable of overcoming physical difficulty since he'd already tested himself in crew.

It was this ability to perform well and maintain focus in the least ideal conditions, along with his high level of personal responsibility, that set Mark apart from others in his field. These qualities made the difference between being a good surgeon and a surgical leader, and he's convinced the training he had in crew permeated almost every area of his professional life. "Being part of the team, getting that ethic of hard work, and focusing so intensely was, to me, something I hadn't really done before outside of athletics," Mark says. "And the career choice I took, neurosurgery, isn't a casual lifestyle. The experience of rowing and being so focused was a real strength as I got through medical school and beyond."

Today, many years after medical school, Mark is known for his incredible sense of personal responsibility, as well as the ability to instill that same level of care in people on his team. In the world of neurosurgery, the stakes are the ultimate—life or death—and mistakes could mean devastating consequences.

One evening, an athlete came to Boston Children's Hospital with a serious spinal cord injury from a football accident. Although Mark was at the hospital that day, he was not directly notified of the injury from the junior resident on his team responsible for the child's care; rather, he learned about it in the emergency room…a couple of hours after the athlete was admitted to the hospital. Mark was immediately concerned about the patient, knowing there was a small sliver of time to save this young athlete from paralysis. Within thirty minutes of hearing about the injury, Mark had the patient in surgery to have his spine decompressed. If much more time had gone by, the patient might have been on a ventilator for the rest of his life, rather than ultimately being able to walk again.

Prioritizing and Leadership

Along with leading by example, Mark believes surgical leaders need to prioritize. "I have seen leaders in my field or in leadership positions who don't lead very well," he says. "They are more interested in making money or taking care of themselves than in taking care of patients or helping to develop the careers of others. Professionalism goes a long way. Part of the role of a physician is to put the interests of the patient in front of your own.

"If you don't put patients first, the patient isn't going to do very well. But more than that, you're teaching the next generation that your interests are more important than the patient's. And that's absolutely the wrong message to send."

The incident made it vividly clear to the person on Mark's team how a lack of prioritizing—or even calling Mark in on the case—could have devastated this young patient's life. Mark uses such cases as learning experiences, as he works to help instill accountability and personal responsibility in the younger surgeons on his team. He wants his residents to "see it from the patient's perspective" and make well-informed decisions quickly. What's essential is caring about the people you're caring for—people whose lives and well-being are at stake.

"What you consider to be your failures gives you the most experience," Mark says. He remembers such a time when he was a junior resident, working every other night on call for six months, thirty-six hours on, twelve hours off. One evening, when he was especially exhausted, a nurse called him several times to ask about a patient with respiratory issues. He made recommendations without getting out of bed, and on morning rounds he found that the patient was very ill. Mark was understandably troubled at the patient's state, since he knew he could have prevented it, had he gotten up to examine her. She ended up doing well, but the case has stuck in Mark's mind for over twenty years, a constant reminder to him of how important it is to give all patients his care and attention—no matter how tired he is. So, with cases like the athlete, Mark knows he can use individual mistakes to teach physicians on his team to better serve many, many more patients.

Not surprisingly, Mark has won over residents and physicians alike at Boston Children's Hospital. He was made the director of residency because the residents like and respect him—they see him as a teacher and mentor, someone who wants them to become the best doctors they can become. And in 2012, without campaigning or even planning to run, he was elected to the prestigious role of president of the Physicians' Organization, a group that includes over 900 physicians. In fact, he was added to the ballot just a few weeks before the elections, his name mostly there as "filler" after another candidate dropped out. While he didn't expect to win—or even compete—he was honored to be selected by so many of his peers. It is evident his peers respect him for his values and high level of personal responsibility, qualities which are a fundamental part of who he is and help define him as a person and surgeon.

In the field of medicine, a small percentage of physicians reach the pinnacle of patient care and hospital/national leadership, which requires both intense effort and teamwork, qualities instilled in rowers from the beginning. From working with younger surgeons to caring deeply for the patients he treats, Mark takes his surgical practice to a new level, giving it his all—just like he did in crew. And the results are well worth the hard work. He has saved lives and improved others, while influencing hundreds of doctors who will go out into the world and do the same.

Advance Through Trust

"If you want to move up in an organization, you need to show yourself to be extremely reliable. People have to trust you. In neurosurgery, that means people have to trust you to take care of patients," Mark explains. "Another way to advance is to set yourself apart in some way. For me, injury prevention is one way I do that."

Whit's Words

Responsibility is a perfect word for a physician in Mark's position and world. Mark is trained to handle high-risk emergency situations that can make the difference between permanent paralysis and walking out of the hospital. He also empowers others around him to have the same level of responsibility. Similarly, when you take personal responsibility, you're holding yourself accountable for the outcomes of your work. Mark's story illustrates the four components that created a successful outcome, just like in the athlete's ability to recover from his serious injury: authority, responsibility, information, and accountability. Are those components present in your work?

Authority: Mark had the authority from his superiors and in his position to make critical decisions that allowed him to save the youth from paralysis. Do you have the authority you need to make proper and timely decisions in your work? As a leader, have you given your direct reports enough authority to make decisions when you aren't available?

Responsibility: Mark was clear about his responsibilities as the surgeon in charge to perform the necessary steps required. Are you clear about what your responsibilities are and what the expectations are within your role? Do you have more responsibility than you have authority? You need to have equal authority to your responsibilities, or you will feel limited in your position.

Information: At first, Mark did not have all the information needed because his colleagues didn't inform him of the patient's serious condition. Do you have all the information needed to make good decisions? If not, what information don't you have, and how could you find that information? Do your direct reports have all the information needed to do their jobs effectively?

Accountability: As Mark exemplified by his response to the athlete with the spinal cord injury, Mark held himself highly accountable to the outcomes of his decisions. It was the same way with crew. He made a decision that he held to and continued showing up for practice every day. Are you holding yourself accountable for your professional responsibilities or are you waiting for others to hold you accountable? As a leader, what metrics are you using to promote high accountability within your department? Do you feel you have to monitor your direct reports' accountability, or could you ask them to come up with their own accountability measures?

In my coaching, I use this simple formula with leaders to help them take the pulse of their direct reports: Empowerment = Authority x Responsibility x Information x Accountability (ARIA). If you want to emulate Mark and improve your empowerment of others, here is an exercise to give you enough information about your team to adjust your leadership style:

Start each question using the rating scale 0–10, with 10 being the highest level.

A = Authority
- How much authority have you been given to do your job to the best of your abilities?

R = Responsibility
- How much responsibility have you been given in your present position?

I = Information
- Do you have all the information you need to do the best job possible in your position?

A = Accountability
- How accountable are you holding yourself (or are you being held by others) to do your job to the best of your abilities?

Here are some ideas to implement the ARIA formula:
1. Do this exercise yourself first. Share your numbers with your boss or your board of directors.

2. Complete a three-by-five card for each of your direct reports before asking them to complete their ratings. See where there are similarities but more importantly gaps between your ratings and their ratings.

3. Look for insights in the gaps between the four attributes. Example: Here are numbers from one of your direct reports. Before looking at my analysis, think about what is going on for this person. As a leader, what are you doing that's creating these numbers and what can you do to improve these ratings?
   $A = 6, R = 9, I = 4, A = 10$

   Analysis:
   You have an employee who has been given more responsibility than authority, without enough information to make good decisions and is being held to a high level of accountability.
   This information should give you good information for much better communication and productivity.

Mark's high level of responsibility started well before his years in surgery; he practiced responsibility and held himself accountable for getting to practice each day during his four years as an oarsman at Dartmouth. He won an award, not for being the most talented oarsman, but for holding himself accountable and being responsible in his training and involvement with the team.

Mark showed me how much being a part of the '86 crew meant to him by showing up at the boathouse to row twenty-five years after his graduation. He was proud to introduce his wife and kids to me during reunion weekend, and I was proud to have supported him in the sport twenty-five years earlier. It's amazing to think about what crew did for Mark and the other oarsmen at Dartmouth. Without the impact of crew and the experiences of the team members, this book would not have been written. Learning to work in sync has forever impacted the crew's personal and professional lives.

Conclusion

Here it is—we have come full circle together. When I started interviewing and writing, the idea seemed so simple: take the stories of eleven Ivy League athletes and draw analogies from what they learned out on the water to what they've accomplished in their personal and professional lives over the past twenty-five years. But what started out as a simple idea ended up as a series of complex, inspiring lessons from eleven outstanding men.

The crew season ended in early June on Lake Onondaga in Syracuse, New York. It was the Intercollegiate Rowing Association's National Championship Regatta. I had started the season teaching these athletes basics, like how to put the shell into the water and how to step into the boat without stepping *through* the boat. Our work together began with long rows in the fall, learning how to get the oar into and out of the water cleanly. The hard training continued with many hours spent indoors, lifting weights and rowing in the indoor tanks and rowing ergometers. The grueling ten-mile runs through the snow and ice in mid-February gave them tolerance for pain, and traveling to Tennessee in the early spring to get miles and miles of water time prepared them for the Yale race. They learned how to get a one-ton racing shell up and moving at full speed with synchronicity and power in less than twenty strokes. The aching bodies, bloodied hands, bursting lungs, nervous emotions, pain of losing, and the joy of winning—all for a six-minute race.

Now, they were sitting at the starting line of their final 2000-meter race with over thirty crews from the likes of the University of Washington, the US Naval Academy, the University of Pennsylvania, and Boston University. It was amazing how much they'd learned and grown throughout the season. I was so proud of them. Here they were putting it all together for the National Championship Regatta. Could they do it? I heard and felt my heart pounding at the starting line, waiting on my bike on shore for the starter's commands, and I imagined what the young athletes must have been experiencing at the same time:

"Are you ready?" *Is my oar buried in the water? Am I sitting up tall at the catch?*
"Ready all." *Relax. Breathe. Put it all together right here and now for the next six minutes.*
"Row!" *We're off!*

You have had the great pleasure of reading about eleven champions in their own right. They started as a very young and inexperienced team back in September of 1982; today, they are successful fathers, brothers, husbands, entrepreneurs, risk takers, caretakers, teachers, service providers, and teammates. Each of their stories details what they learned about sport, about pushing past the limits of pain, about camaraderie, about selflessness, about teamwork, and about friendship.

It's your turn now. What would you challenge yourself to do differently in your work or personal life? Which story might you want to revisit? What did you identify with or learn that you might want to try in your own life?

Imagine sitting in a sixty-one-foot shell that only weighs about 220 pounds, with your feet strapped in and your hands holding onto the end of a twelve-foot oar. You've just been pushed out into the river for your first row upstream. Now, what are you supposed to do? The boat is really tippy, the current is running by you, and the guys behind you and in front of you don't know any more about what's about to happen than you do. Maybe if you just listen to the coach or the coxswain, you will feel more secure in this new environment.

Nine months later, you are sitting on the starting line of the National Championship Regatta with crews from across the country on either side. How is this scenario like your work? What do you need to do to get down that course faster than all those crews—teams that have been through the same pain, hard work, success, and failure? Will it be what you learned from your mentor, coach, direct report, peer, or boss? How can you beat that competition? How hard do you have to pull? Will you make it down the course without catching a crab? Can you depend on your teammates to pull just as hard? What is the trophy at the end of the race?

If you want to put yourself into that tippy shell and see what you can learn and do differently, then step up the edge of the dock and pick your spot. Your seat is open. Step gently without fear. Hold the end of the oar as you take your seat. And then do the most important command—listen!

Practice Time

Which workout would you like to put into practice today? Pick one and give it a go. Here are some suggestions to help you build courage, endurance, power, skills, and a winning crew:

1. Ask each member of your leadership team to read *Working in Sync*. Each month or quarter, pick one chapter to discuss in a meeting as part of your professional development.

2. Ask each leader to pick one chapter and present their insights and learning with a call to action to the team.

3. Pick a chapter for your team to focus on over the next thirty, sixty, or ninety days. Master the skills, behaviors, or leadership attributes illustrated in the chapter.

4. Pick a peer coach and read *Working in Sync* over a thirty-day period. Identify one area for mastery, and inform your peer coach what he or she could do to support and encourage you through that change process.

5. Work with an executive coach to identify a chapter that illustrates one of the areas where you have the greatest growth potential. Expand your knowledge and understanding of your own abilities with your coach. Set a plan in place with accountability measures.

6. Buy copies of *Working in Sync,* and send them to the people in your life who have made a difference. Thank them for their time, care, patience, and love. Put together a list of past coaches, teachers, pastors, relatives, colleagues, and friends who have impacted you.

Acknowledgments

To my coaches:

Chick Willing, South Kent School, Head Rowing Coach: With a balanced sense of humor and strong work ethic, Chick could take mediocre athletes and create champions.

Bill Stowe, Litchfield Rowing Association and US Coast Guard Academy, Head Rowing Coach: "Never jump the start but always get to the finish line first!" Taught me how to make hard work fun.

Bill Pickard, Dartmouth College, Head Woman's Coach: I have never met anyone that is as passionate about crew as Bill.

Peter Gardner, Dartmouth College, Head Men's Rowing Coach: Was known by all as "Coach." Was a quiet force who taught me to listen, taught me to be open to suggestions, and taught me to enjoy the time on the river.

John Kerrick, Peer Coach: My accountability coach, every week for fifteen minutes for the past six years. High value for so little time.

Mark LeBlanc, Small Business Success, Author, Speaker, Coach: A master presenter and past president of the National Speakers Association, Mark gave me the courage, systems, and support to "start and grow" my own small business. A true friend who believes in me.

Ron Price, Price Associates, Strategist, Consultant, Coach, Entrepreneur, Partner: Ron shined the light down the path of confidence and wisdom and gave me the keys that unlocked my creative spirit, leading to greater happiness and peace of mind. Ron's intellect, business expertise, and spiritual wisdom played a large role in getting this book to completion.

Thanks to all the Dartmouth class of '86 team members who were so gracious with their time.

To my book family:

Stacy Ennis, Editor and Book Visionary: Stacy is the person with the words behind the mirror. She put her professional expertise into crafting my words and the words of the eleven Dartmouth athletes into this story. Her patience, attention to the details, well-timed questions, and personal friendship have led to a higher quality story.

Maryanna Young, Publisher, Project Visionary, and Team Leader: Maryanna met me one afternoon in Boise, Idaho, listened to my story, and jumped at the idea. Her vision, never-ending encouragement, past athletic experiences, wonderful wisdom, and calm confidence created a year to remember…always!

Thank you also to the Aloha Publishing team who was so helpful every step of the way: Kelly Cope, book outline strategist; Cari Campbell, the most patient cover designer ever; Nick Zelinger, interior designer with NZ Graphics; Merilee Marsh, Hannah Cross, Kim Foster, fact checkers, and final edit team; and Justin Foster and Jeremy Billups with branding concepts and strategy. There are so many others who made *Working in Sync* possible. Thank you from the depth of my heart.

To my family:

E. Whitney Mitchell, Dad: Dad had a picture of the Cornell Crew that he rowed on in 1948 sitting behind his desk. He was six feet two inches and rowed in the bow seat of that freshman eight. He loved taking me to sporting events.

Barb Hills: Barb and I were a coaching team, coaching together at UNH, the US Coast Guard Academy, and Dartmouth College. An exquisite rowing coach and mother, she continues to pursue her crew coaching passion in Camden, Maine.

Lizzie Mitchell, Daughter: Rowed at the University of Vermont. An adventurist who loves people, loves to laugh, and loves to ski. Is determined to make the world a better place to live.

Ry Mitchell, Daughter: Sailed at the University of Vermont. Ry is a coach, an artist, an athlete, and an exceptional sailor. Ry has the innate ability to know when to connect with others who need her most.

Whitter Mitchell, Son: A hockey player and NH State Champion. A sensitive and kind human being, always looking out for the other person. A sports enthusiast and my partner at many Boston sporting events.

Judy Coates, Wife and lifelong friend: Judy has given me the gifts of reflection and patience. Her continued words of encouragement and thought-provoking questions helped me write with more purpose, intent, and feelings. She has a way of bringing out my soul and my values while allowing me to be me!

About the Author

Whit Mitchell is an executive coach specializing in team dynamics. He is the founder and CEO of Working InSync International. Over the past 30 years, Whit has worked with a diverse group of executives across Fortune 500 companies, regional corporations, and small businesses, developing dynamic leaders and teams.

In addition to his expertise in team development, Whit has worked with top executive development programs at Tuck School of Business, Harvard University, and Columbia University. His work with collegiate and professional athletes and coaches includes Dartmouth College, the US Coast Guard Academy, the University of New Hampshire, and professional hockey players.

Whit and his wife, Judy, live with their yellow lab, Kyla, in Hanover, New Hampshire.

If you want to learn more about Whit's availability to help you or your organization, you can contact him at whit@workinginsync.com.